CW01020424

Texts in Computing

Volume 16

Implementing
Programming
Languages

An Introduction to
Compilers and Interpreters

Texts in Computing Series Editor
Ian Mackie   mackie@lix.polytechnique

Implementing Programming Languages

An Introduction to Compilers and Interpreters

Aarne Ranta

with an appendix coauthored by

Markus Forsberg

Aarne Ranta is Professor of Computer Science at the University of Gothenburg, Sweden. He has lectured on programming language technology since 2002 and been the leader or supervisor of several language implementation projects. The most important ones are the GF formalism for natural language processing and the BNFC tool for compiler construction.

Markus Forsberg is a Researcher in Language Technology at the University of Gothenburg. Together with Ranta, he wrote the first implementation of BNFC.

ISBN 978-1-84890-064-6

College Publications
Scientific Director: Dov Gabbay
Managing Director: Jane Spurr
Department of Computer Science
King's College London, Strand, London WC2R 2LS, UK

http://www.collegepublications.co.uk

Original cover design by Richard Fraser
Cover produced by Laraine Welch
Printed by Lightning Source, Milton Keynes, UK

Contents

Preface

This book is an introduction to programming language technology and compiler construction. It is different from traditional compiler books in several ways:

- It is much thinner, yet covers all the techniques needed for typical tasks.

- It has more pure theory (semantics, inference rules) but also a fair amount of actual practice (how to write code).

- It leaves low-level details to standard tools whenever available.

If you can invest full-time work to this book, you should be able to learn the material in a couple of weeks, which includes completing the programming assignments. This covers the complete chain from source code to machine code: lexing, parsing, type checking, code generators, and interpreters. With the knowledge gained, you can later build your own languages as a matter of days, sometimes even hours.

The book follows a **theory-based practical approach**. This means that the ultimate goal is to write programs that work, but the best way to achieve this is via theoretical thinking. Thus we will specify each compiler component first by theoretical concepts such as grammars and inference rules. Then we will show how the theory is converted to practice, often by mechanically translating the description into program code. Theory thus works as blueprint for the code.

The goal is to get you quickly into the business of actually implementing a language and running programs written in it. This exercise serves two purposes:

1. You will understand better than before how existing languages work.

2. You will learn skills needed for creating new languages,

To further support these goals, there are a few theory chapters and sections, which are marked with an asterisk (*). These parts can perhaps be left out if you are only interested in the latter goal. But of course, to talk with any authority about compilers, the knowledge of the underlying theory is essential. The theory sections try to make this interesting and relevant, by giving answers to questions that are likely to arise even in practice, such as:

- Why don't most languages allow nested comments?

- What exactly can be done in a parser?

- Why can't a compiler detect all errors in programs?

- Will the compiler improve my lousy programs by optimization?

- How simple can a language be? And how close could it be to human language?

Aimed as a first book on the topic, this is not a substitute for the "real" books if you want to do research in compilers, or if you are involved in cutting edge implementations of large programming languages. Some of the many things that we have left out are low-level details of lexer implementation, algorithms for building LR parser generators, data flow analysis, register allocation, memory management, and parallelism. The lexer and parser details are left out because they are nowadays handled by standard tools, and application programmers can concentrate on just specifying their own languages and leave the details to the tools. The other aspects are left out because they are handled by standard back ends such as the Java Virtual Machine and LLVM. Appendix D of the book gives reading hints on the more advanced topics.

How to use this book

The text runs in parallel with practical programming work, which is divided to six assignments. You cannot claim really to have read this book unless you have yourself completed these assignments:

1. A grammar and parser for a fragment of C++.

2. A type checker for a smaller fragment of C++, to be called CPP.

3. An interpreter for CPP.

4. A compiler from CPP to Java Virtual Machine (JVM).

5. An interpreter for a functional language: a fragment of Haskell, to be called Fun.

6. The design and implementation of a domain-specific language.

The language CPP is a small part of the immense language C++; we could almost as well say C or Java. However, the parser (Assignment 1) also contains many of the tricky special features of C++ such as templates. The purpose of this is to throw you into cold water and show that you can actually swim.

Managing to do this assignment will give you confidence that you can easily cope with *any* feature of programming language syntax.

Assignments 2, 3, and 4 deal with a small language, which however contains everything that is needed for writing useful programs: arithmetic expressions, declarations and assignments, conditionals, loops, blocks, functions, strings, input and output. They will give the basic understanding of how programming languages work. Most features of imperative programming languages can then be understood as variations of the same themes. Assignment 5 widens the perspective by introducing the concepts of functional programming, such as higher-order functions and closures.

The assignments are not only practical but also close to the "real world". Compiler books sometimes use toy languages and home-made virtual machines, in order to focus on the pure concepts rather than messy details. But we have preferred fragments of real languages (C++, Haskell) and a real virtual machine (JVM). Even though some details of these languages might be messy, they have a core that we find pure enough to give a good representation of the concepts.

The advantage of using real languages is that you can easily compare your work with standard compilers. You can for instance produce your own Java class files and link them together with files generated by standard Java compilers. When running your code, you will probably experience the embarrassment (and pleasure!) of seeing things like bytecode verification errors, which rarely arise with standard compilers! To give even more perspective, we will show the basics of compilation to Intel x86 code, which will enable you to compile and run some simple programs "on bare silicon".

The assignments require you to write code in two different formats:

- a grammar formalism: BNFC (= BNF Converter; BNF = Backus Naur Form),

- a general-purpose programming language: Java or Haskell.

Thus you don't need to write code for traditional compiler tools such as Lex and Yacc. Such code, as well as many other parts of the compiler, are automatically derived from the BNFC grammar. For the general-purpose language, you could actually choose any of Java, Haskell, C, C++, C#, or OCaml, since BNFC supports all these languages. But in this book, we will focus on the use of Java and Haskell as implementation language. You should choose the language according to your taste and experience. If you want to use C++ or C#, you can easily follow the Java code examples, whereas OCaml programmers can follow Haskell. C is a little different, but mostly closer to Java than to Haskell. The theory-based approach guarantees that very little in the material is tied to a specific implementation language: since the compiler components are explained on an abstract level, they can be easily implemented in different languages.

Assignment 6, domain-specific language, is more open-ended but builds on the methods learnt in the previous tasks. It is supported by Chapter 8, which also puts language design into a historical and theoretical perspective. The history of programming languages shows a steady development towards higher-level languages—in a sense, coming closer and closer to human language. This is an area with a lot of future potential. Applications such as speech-based human-computer interaction and automatic translation are getting common-place. We will emphasize the relevance of programming language techniques for these tasks, without forgetting the differences and unsolved problems.

In addition to the assignments, the book has some exercises. Most of them target the theoretical extra material, since the main material is well covered by the assignments. Some exercises require hours or even days of work and are marked with a plus (+).

Web resources

This book has a web page,

> http://digitalgrammars.com/ipl-book/

This web page contains

- the complete specifications of the six assignments

- associated code templates and test suites

- slides for teaching from this book

- solutions to some exercises

- links to useful software

- links to on-line reference publications

- errata

Teaching from this book

This book is based on ten years of lecturing on programming language tech-nology and compiler construction at Chalmers University of Technology and the University of Gothenburg. I have covered most of the material in a quarter year's course at half pace, which corresponds to four weeks of full-time study or 7.5 European credit points. The students have been partly from an engineering track (about two thirds), partly from a science curriculum (about a third). The range of students has been from second-year Bachelor to fourth-year Masters students.

Bachelor level students have completed Assignments 1 to 3 (parser, type checker, interpreter), corresponding to Chapters 1 to 5. Master level students have also completed Assignment 5 (functional language interpreter), whereas Assignment 4 (JVM generation) is left to a special course on compiler back ends. Chapters 6 to 8 have however been covered in a cursory fashion by lectures and exercises on all levels.

We have used one two-hour lecture for the theoretical material of each chapter. In addition, we have given "coding lectures" for each assignment, where the teacher writes some code in interaction with the students to show how to get started with the work. Some years I have indulged in an entire extra lecture on "compiling natural language" (Chapter 8), reflecting my research interests. Other teachers might similarly spend more time on for instance optimization (Chapter 6) or advanced type systems (Chapter 7).

The prerequisites for signing up at the course have been minimal: programming skills and basic data structures (lists, trees, symbol table representations). No particular programming language has been required; in practice, around half of the students have made their assignments in Haskell, the other half in Java, with some occasional C++ and C submissions. Of course, understanding the tasks in Assignments 2 to 4 requires a reading knowledge of an imperative language, and Assignment 5 is easier for those with functional programming experience. Some knowledge of symbolic logic is also useful but not necessary.

We haven't observed any radical difference between Java and Haskell programmers' performance. Except the most experienced ones, both kinds of programmers will have to learn some new techniques. In Java, this is the **visitor pattern**, to implement **pattern matching**, which for Haskell programmers comes for free. In Haskell, **monads** will be needed for a smooth treatment of **side effects** such as changing the environment; these in turn are trivial for Java programmers. Thus neither language is clearly the ultimate choice for compiler writing, which is yet another argument for keeping the presentation abstract and language-neutral.

Acknowledgements

Since I first lectured on compiler construction in 2002, more than a thousand students have followed the courses and contributed to the evolution of this material. I am grateful to all the students for useful feedback and for a confirmation that the chosen approach makes sense.

I also want to thank my course assistants throughout these years: Grégoire Détrez, Arnar Birgisson, Ramona Enache, Krasimir Angelov, Michał Pałka, Jean-Philippe Bernardy, Kristoffer Hedberg, Anders Mörtberg, Daniel Hedin,

Håkan Burden, Kuchi Prasad, Björn Bringert, and Josef Svenningsson. They have helped consolidate the material and come with new ideas, in particular for the exercises and assignments in this book. Björn Bringert wrote the code that the Java examples in Chapters 4 and 5 are based on.

The book owes a lot to lecture notes written by earlier teachers of the courses: Ulf Norell, Marcin Benke, Thomas Hallgren, Lennart Augustsson, Thomas Jonsson, and Niklas Röjemo. Thus I have profited from first-rate experience in programming language design and implementation, proven in both large-scale implementations and scientific publications. The spirit of this field in Gothenburg is exactly what I call a theory-based practical approach. The language CPP is based on the language Javalette inherited from earlier courses.

The BNF Converter started as joint work with Markus Forsberg in 2002. In 2003, Michael Pellauer joined the project and created the first versions of C, C++, and Java back ends, making BNFC multilingual. Markus's PhD thesis from 2007 has been one of the main sources of documentation of BNFC, and he has helped in adapting one of our co-authored reports into an appendix of this book: the quick reference manual to BNFC (Appendix A).

Over the years, BNFC has also received substantial contributions (such as back ends for new languages) from Krasimir Angelov, Björn Bringert, Johan Broberg, Paul Callaghan, Ola Frid, Peter Gammie, Patrik Jansson, Kristofer Johannisson, Antti-Juhani Kaijanaho, and Ulf Norell. Many users of BNFC have sent valuable feedback, proving the claim that one of the most precious resources of a piece of software are its users.

A draft of this book was read by Rodolphe Lepigre and Jan Smith, who made many corrections and valuable suggestions. Jane Spurr at King's College Publications was always responsive with accurate editorial help.

Gothenburg, 7 May 2012

Aarne Ranta
aarne@chalmers.se

Chapter 1

Compilation Phases

This chapter introduces the concepts and terminology for most of the later discussion. It explains the difference between compilers and interpreters, the division into low and high level languages, and the data structures and algorithms involved in each component of a programming language implementation. Many of these components are known as the **compilation phases**, that is, the phases through which a compiler goes on its way from source code to machine code.

1.1 From language to binary

As everyone knows, computers manipulate 0's and 1's. This is done by the help of electric circuits, where 0 means no current goes through and 1 means that it does. The reason why this is useful is that so many things can be expressed by using just 0's and 1's—by **bit sequences**, also known as **binary encoding**. In the mathematical theory of information, one goes as far as to say that **information** is the same thing as bit sequences. One way to make sense of this is to think about information in terms of yes/no questions. A sequence of answers to enough many questions can specify any object. For instance, a popular game in my childhood was one in which one player thought about a person and the other tried to guess who it was by asking maximally 20 yes/no questions.

The first thing to encode in binary are the integers:

```
0 = 0
1 = 1
2 = 10
3 = 11
4 = 100
```

and so on. This generalizes easily to letters and to other characters, for instance by the use of the ASCII encoding:

```
A = 65 = 1000001
B = 66 = 1000010
C = 67 = 1000011
```

and so on. In this way we can see that all **data** manipulated by computers can be expressed by 0's and 1's. But what is crucial is that even the **programs** that manipulate the data can be so expressed. To take a real-world example, programs in the JVM machine language (**Java Virtual Machine**) are sequences of **bytes**, that is, groups of eight 0's or 1's (capable of expressing the numbers from 0 to 255). A byte can encode a numeric value, for instance an integer or a character as above. But it can also encode an **instruction**, that is, a command to do something. For instance, addition and multiplication (of integers) are expressed in JVM as bytes in the following way:

```
+ =   96 = 0110 0000 = 60
* = 104 = 0110 1000 = 68
```

We put a space in the middle of each byte to make it more readable, and more spaces between bytes. The last figure shown is a **hexadecimal** encoding, where each half-byte is encoded by a base-16 digit that ranges from 0 to F (with A=10, B=11,...,F=15). Hexadecimals are a common way to display binaries in machine language documentation.

From the encodings of numbers and operators, one could construct a simple-minded encoding of arithmetic formulas, by just putting together the codes for 5, +, and 6:

```
5 + 6 = 0000 0101    0110 0000    0000 0110
```

While this could be made to work, actual JVM chooses a more roundabout way. In the logic that it follows, the expression is first converted to a **postfix** form, where the operands come before the operator:

$$5 + 6 \Longrightarrow 5\ 6\ +$$

One virtue of the postfix form is that we don't need parentheses. For instance,

$$(5 + 6) * 7 \Longrightarrow 5\ 6\ +\ 7\ *$$
$$5 + (6 * 7) \Longrightarrow 5\ 6\ 7\ *\ +$$

At least the former expression needs parentheses when the usual **infix** order is used, that is, when the operator is between the operands.

The way the JVM machine manipulates expressions is based on a so-called **stack**, which is the working memory of the machine. The stack is like a pile of plates, where new plates are **pushed** on the stack, and only one plate is available at a time, the one last pushed—known as the **top** of the stack. An arithmetic operation such as + (usually called "add") takes the two top-most elements from the stack and returns their sum on the top. Thus the computation of, say, 5 + 6, proceeds as follows, where the left column shows the instructions and the right column the stack after each instruction:

```
bipush 5  ;  5
bipush 6  ;  5 6
iadd      ;  11
```

The instructions are here shown as **assembly code**, which means that readable instruction names and decimal numbers are used instead of binaries. The instruction `bipush` means pushing an integer that has the size of one byte, and `iadd` means integer addition.

To take a more complex example, the computation of 5 + (6 * 7) is

```
bipush 5  ; 5
bipush 6  ; 5 6
bipush 7  ; 5 6 7
imul      ; 5 42
iadd      ; 47
```

In this case, unlike the previous one, the stack at one point contains more numbers than two; but the integer multiplication (`imul`) instruction correctly picks the topmost ones 6 and 7 and returns the value 42 on the stack.

The binary JVM code must make it clear which bytes stand for numeric values and which ones for instructions such as "add". This is obvious if you think that we need to read 0110 0000 sometimes as number 96, and sometimes as addition. The way to make it clear that a byte stands for a numeric value is to prefix it with a special instruction, the one called `bipush`. Thus we get the code for an addition expression:

5 + 6 $\Longrightarrow$ bipush 5 bipush 6 iadd

To convert this all into binary, we only need the code for the push instruction,

```
bipush = 16 = 0001 0000
```

Now we can express the entire arithmetic expression as binary:

5 + 6 = 0001 0000 0000 0101 0001 0000 0000 0110 0110 0000

We hope to have made two important things clear now:

- Both data and programs can be expressed as binary code, i.e. by 0's and 1's.

- There is a systematic translation from conventional ("user-friendly") expressions to binary code.

Of course we will need more instructions to represent variables, assignments, loops, functions, and other constructs found in programming languages, but the principles are the same as in the simple example above. The translation from program code to binary is the very task of the program called a **compiler**. The compiler from arithmetic expressions to JVM byte code works as follows:

1. Analyse the expression into an operator F and its operands X and Y.

2. Compile the code for X, followed by the code for Y, followed by the code for F.

This procedure is our first example of a compiler. It shows the two main ideas of compilers, which we will repeat again and again in new configurations:

1. **Syntactic analysis**: here, to find the main operator of an expression, and then analyse its operands.

2. **Syntax-directed translation**: the compiler calls the compiler on the operands of the expression, and combines the resulting code with the code for the operator. This is iterated until the simplest parts are reached (here, the numeric constants).

Both syntactic analysis and syntax-directed translation use **recursion**: they are functions that call themselves on parts of the expression.

Exercise 1-0. Show the assembly code and the binary and hexadecimal JVM encoding of the expression

$$11 + 7 * (9 + 5)$$

Also show the evolution of the stack when the expression is evaluated.

Exercise 1-1. Decode the following representation of a JVM program to show (a) the corresponding assembly code and (b) a Java expression from which it can be obtained.

```
0001 0000 1111 1111 0001 0000 0010 0000
0110 0000 0001 0000 0000 1001 0110 1000
```

A list of the most important JVM codes can be found in Appendix B.

_____ human

human language

ML   Haskell

Lisp   Prolog

C++   Java

C

assembler

machine language

_____ machine

Figure 1.1: Some programming languages from the highest to the lowest level.

1.2 Levels of languages

The task of a compiler may be more or less demanding. This depends on the distance of the languages it translates between. The situation is related to translation between human languages: it is easier to translate from English to French than from English to Japanese, because French is closer to English than Japanese is, both in the family tree of languages and because of cultural influences.

But the meaning of "closer" is clearer in the case of computer languages. Often it is directly related to the **level** of the language. The binary machine language is usually defined as the *lowest* level, whereas the highest level might be human language such as English. Usual programming languages are between these levels, as shown by the diagram in Figure 1.1. The diagram is very sketchy. C++, for instance, is a language that reaches both the low level of C (with its memory management, cf. Section 5.8) and the high level of Lisp (with higher order functions, cf. Section 7.2).

Because of their distance to the machine, **high-level languages** are more difficult to compile than **low-level languages**. Notice that "high" and "low" don't imply any value judgements here; the idea is simply that higher levels are closer to human thought, whereas lower levels are closer to the operation of machines. Both humans and machines are needed to make computers work in the way we are used to. Some people might claim that only the lowest level of binary code is necessary, because humans can be trained to write it. But to this one can object that programmers could never write very sophisticated programs by using machine code only—they could just not keep the millions of bytes needed in their heads. Therefore, it is usually much more productive to write high-level code and let a compiler produce the binary.

The history of programming languages indeed shows a steady progress from lower to higher levels. Programmers can usually be more productive when writing in high-level languages, which means that high levels are desirable; at the same time, raising the level implies a challenge to compiler writers. Thus the evolution of programming languages goes hand in hand with developments in compiler technology. It has of course also helped that the machines have become more powerful. Compilation can be a heavy computation task, and the computers of the 1960's could not have run the compilers of the 2010's. Moreover, it is harder to write compilers that produce efficient code than ones that waste some resources.

Here is a very rough list of programming languages in the history, only mentioning ones that have implied something new in terms of programming language expressivity:

- 1940's: connecting wires to represent 0's and 1's

- 1950's: assemblers, macro assemblers, Fortran, COBOL, Lisp

- 1960's: ALGOL, BCPL ($\rightarrow$ B $\rightarrow$ C), SIMULA

- 1970's: Smalltalk, Prolog, ML

- 1980's: C++, Perl, Python

- 1990's: Haskell, Java

1.3   Compilation and interpretation

In a way, a compiler reverses the history of programming languages. What we saw before goes from a "1960's" source language:

```
5 + 6 * 7
```

to a "1950's" assembly language

```
bipush 5 bipush 6 bipush 7 imul iadd
```

and further to a "1940's" machine language

```
0001 0000   0000 0101   0001 0000   0000 0110
0001 0000   0000 0111   0110 1000   0110 0000
```

The second step is very easy: you just look up the binary codes for each symbol in the assembly language and put them together in the same order. It is sometimes not regarded as a part of compilation proper, but as a separate level of **assembly**. The main reason for this is purely practical: modern compilers don't need to go all the way to the binary, but just to the assembly language, since there exist assembly programs that can do the rest.

A compiler is a program that **translates** code to some other code. It does not actually run the program. An **interpreter** does this. Thus a source language expression,

```
5 + 6 * 7
```

is by an interpreter turned to its value,

```
47
```

This computation can be performed without any translation of the source code into machine code. However, a common practice is in fact a *combination* of compilation and interpretation. For instance, Java programs are, as shown above, compiled into JVM code. This code is in turn interpreted by a JVM interpreter.

The compilation of Java is different from for instance the way C is translated by GCC (GNU Compiler Collection). GCC compiles C into the native code of each machine, which is just executed, not interpreted. JVM code must be interpreted because it is not executable by any actual machine.

Sometimes a distinction is made between "compiled languages" and "interpreted languages", C being compiled and Java being interpreted. This is really a misnomer, in two ways. First, *any* language could have both an interpreter and a compiler. Second, it's not Java that is interpreted by a "Java interpreter", but JVM, a completely different language to which Java is compiled.

Here are some examples of how some known languages are normally treated:

- C is usually compiled to machine code by GCC.

- Java is usually compiled to JVM bytecode by Javac, and this bytecode is usually interpreted, although parts of it can be compiled to machine code by **JIT** (**just in time compilation**).

- JavaScript is interpreted in web browsers.

- Unix shell scripts are interpreted by the shell.

- Haskell programs are either compiled to machine code using GHC, or to bytecode interpreted in Hugs or GHCI.

Compilation vs. interpretation is one of the important decisions to make when designing and implementing a new language. Here are some trade-offs:

Advantages of interpretation:

- faster to get going

- easier to implement

- portable to different machines

Advantages of compilation:

- if to machine code: the resulting code is faster to execute

- if to machine-independent target code: the resulting code is easier to interpret than the source code

The advent of JIT is blurring the distinction, and so do virtual machines with actual machine language instruction sets, such as VMWare. In general, the best trade-offs are achieved by combinations of compiler and interpreter components, reusing as much as possible (as we saw is done in the reuse of the assembly phase). This leads us to the following topic: how compilers are divided into separate components.

1.4   Compilation phases

A compiler even for a simple language easily becomes a complex program, which is best attacked by dividing it to smaller components. These components typically address different **compilation phases**. Each phase is a part of a pipeline, which transforms the code from one format to another. These formats are typically encoded in different data structures: each phase returns a data structure that is easy for the next phase to manipulate.

The diagram in Figure 1.2 shows the main compiler phases and how a piece of source code travels through them. The code is on the left, the down-going arrows are annotated by the names of the phases, and the data structure is on the right. Here are some more words of explanation:

- The **lexer** reads a string of **characters** and chops it into **tokens**, i.e. to "meaningful words"; the figure represents the token string by putting spaces between tokens.

- The **parser** reads a string of tokens and groups it into a **syntax tree**, i.e. to a structure indicating which parts belong together and how; the figure represents the syntax tree by using parentheses.

- The **type checker** finds out the **type** of each part of the syntax tree that might have alternative types, and returns an **annotated syntax tree**; the figure represents the annotations by the letter i ("integer") in square brackets.

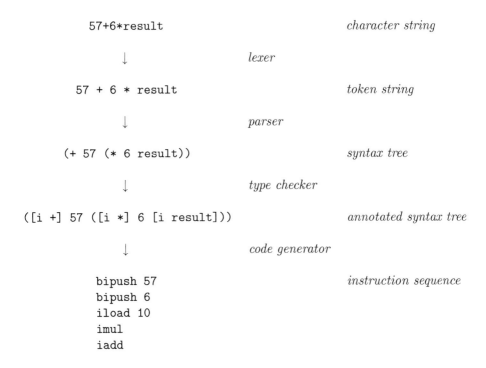

Figure 1.2: Compilation phases from Java source code to JVM assembly code.

- The **code generator** converts the annotated syntax tree into a list of target code instructions. The figure uses normal JVM assembly code, where `imul` means integer multiplication, `bipush` pushing integer bytes, and `iload` pushing values of integer variables.

We want to point out the role of type checking in particular. In a Java-to-JVM compiler it is an indispensable phase in order to perform **instruction selection** in the code generator. The JVM target language has different instructions for the addition of integers and floats, for instance (`iadd` vs. `dadd`), whereas the Java source language uses the same symbol + for both. The type checker analyses the code to find the types of the operands of + to decide whether integer or double addition is needed.

The difference between compilers and interpreters is just in the last phase: interpreters don't generate new code, but execute the old code. However, even then they must perform the earlier phases, which are independent of what the last step will be. This is with the exception of the type checker: compilers tend to require more type checking than interpreters, to enable instruction selection. It is no coincidence that untyped languages such as JavaScript and Python tend to be interpreted languages.

1.5   Compilation errors

Each compiler phases has both a positive and a negative side, so to say. The positive side is that it converts the code to something that is more useful for the next phase, for instance, a token string into a syntax tree. The negative side is that it may fail, in which case it might report an error to the user.

Each compiler phase has its characteristic errors. Here are some examples:

- **Lexer errors**, e.g. unclosed quote,

  ```
  "hello
  ```

- **Parse errors**, e.g. mismatched parentheses,

  ```
  (4 * (y + 5) - 12))
  ```

- **Type errors**, e.g. the application of a function to an argument of wrong kind,

  ```
  sort(45)
  ```

Errors on later phases than type checking are usually not supported. One reason is the principle (by Robin Milner, the creator of ML), that "well-typed programs cannot go wrong". This means that if a program passes the type checker it will also work on later phases. Another, more general reason is that the compiler phases can be divided into two groups:

- The **front end**, which performs **analysis**, i.e. inspects the program: lexer, parser, type checker.

- The **back end**, which performs **synthesis**: code generator.

It is natural that only the front end (analysis) phases look for errors.

A good compiler finds all errors at the earliest occasion. Thereby it saves work: it doesn't try to type check code that has parse errors. It is also more useful for the user, because it can then give error messages that go to the very root of the problem.

Of course, compilers cannot find all errors, for instance, all bugs in the program. The problem with an array index out of bounds is a typical example of such errors. However, in general it is better to find errors at **compile time** than at **run time**, and this is one aspect in which compilers are constantly improving. One of the most important lessons of this book will be to understand what is possible to do at compile time and what must be postponed to run time. For instance, array index out of bounds is not possible to detect at compile time, if the index is a variable that gets its value at run time.

Another typical example is the **binding analysis** of variables: if a variable is used in an expression in Java or C, it must have been declared and given a value. For instance, the following function is incorrect in C:

```
int main () {
  printf("%d",x) ;
  }
```

The reason is that x has not been declared, which for instance GCC correctly reports as an error. But the following is correct in C:

```
int main () {
   int x ;
   printf("%d",x) ;
}
```

What is intuitively a problem is that x has not been given a value. In C, however, the variable then gets the value that happens to be in the memory place reserved for it. The corresponding function when compiled in Java would produce the error "variable x might not have been initialized".

As we will see in Chapter 3, binding analysis cannot be performed in a parser, but must be done in the type checker. However, the situation is worse than this. Consider the function

```
int main () {
  int x ;
  if (readInt()) x = 1 ;
  printf("%d",x) ;
}
```

Here x gets a value under a condition. It may be that this condition is impossible to decide at compile time. Hence it is not decidable at compile time if x has a value—neither in the parser, nor in the type checker.

Exercise 1-2. The following C code has around six errors (some of them depend on what you count as an error). Locate the errors and explain at which compiler phase they are (or should be) revealed.

```
/* this is a buggy hello world program

int main ()
{
  int i ;
  int j = k + 1 ;
  int a[] = {1,2,3}
  j = a + 6 ;
  a[4] = 7 ;
  printf(hello world\n) ;
}
```

1.6   More compilation phases

The compiler phases discussed above are the main phases. There can be many more—here are a couple of examples:

Desugaring/normalization: remove **syntactic sugar**, i.e. language constructs that are there to make the language more convenient for programmers, without adding to the expressive power. Such constructs can be removed early in compilation, so that the later phases don't need to deal with them. An example is multiple declarations, which can be reduced to sequences of single declarations:

```
int i, j ; ⟹ int i ; int j ;
```

Desugaring is normally done at the syntax tree level, and it can be inserted as a phase between parsing and type checking. A disadvantage can be, however, that errors arising in type checking then refer to code that the programmer has never written herself, but that has been created by desugaring.

Optimizations: improve the code in some respect. This can be done on many different levels. For instance, **source code optimization** may precompute values known at compile time:

```
i = 5 + 6 * 7 ; ⟹ i = 47 ;
```

Target code optimization may replace instructions with cheaper ones:

```
bipush 31 bipush 31 ⟹ bipush 31 dup
```

Here the second `bipush 31` is replaced by `dup`, which duplicates the top of the stack. The gain is that the `dup` instruction is just one byte, whereas `bipush 31` is two bytes.

Modern compilers may have dozens of phases. For instance, GCC has several optimization phases performed on the level of **intermediate code**. This code is neither the source nor the target code, but something in between. The advantage of intermediate code is that it makes the components reusable: the same optimizations phases can be combined with different source and target languages.

1.7 Theory and practice

The complex task of compiler writing is greatly helped by the division into phases. Each phase is simple enough to be understood properly; and implementations of different phases can be recombined to new compilers. But there is yet another aspect: many of the phases have a clean mathematical *theory*, which applies to that phase. The following table summarizes those theories:

phase	theory
lexer	finite automata
parser	context-free grammars
type checker	type systems
interpreter	operational semantics
code generator	compilation schemes

The theories provide **declarative notations** for each of the phases, so that they can be specified in clean ways, independently of implementation and usually much more concisely. They will also enable **reasoning** about the compiler components. For instance, the way parsers are written by means of context-free grammars can be used for guaranteeing that the language is *unambiguous*, that is, that each program can be compiled in a unique way.

Syntax-directed translation is a common name for the techniques used in type checkers, interpreters, and code generators alike. We will see that these techniques have so much in common that, once you learn how to implement a type checker, the other components are easy variants of this.

1.8   The scope of the techniques

The techniques of compiler construction are by no means restricted to the traditional task of translating programming language to machine language. The target of the translation can also be another programming language— for instance, the Google Web Toolkit is a compiler from Java into JavaScript, enabling the construction of web applications in a higher-level and type-checked language.

Actually, the modular way in which modern compilers are built implies that it is seldom necessary to go all the way to the machine code (or assembler), even if this is the target. A popular way of building native code compilers is via a translation to C. As soon as C code is reached, the compiler for the new language is complete.

The modularity of compilers also enables the use of compiler components to other tasks, such as debuggers, documentation systems, and code analysis of different kinds. But there is still a reason to learn the whole chain from source language to machine language: it will help you to decide which phases your task resembles the most, and thereby which techniques are the most useful ones to apply.

Chapter 2

Grammars

This chapter is a hands-on introduction to BNFC, the BNF Converter. It explains step by step how to write a grammar, how to convert it into a lexer and a parser, how to test it, and how to solve some problems that are likely to arise with BNFC.

This chapter provides all the concepts and tools needed for solving Assignment 1, which is a parser for a fragment of C++.

2.1 Defining a language

In school teaching, **grammars** are systems of rules used for teaching languages. They specify how words are formed (e.g. that the plural of the noun *baby* is *babies*) and how words are combined to sentences (e.g. that in English the subject usually appears before the verb). Grammars can be more or less complete, and people who actually speak a language may follow the grammar more or less strictly. In **linguistics**, where grammars are studied in a scientific way, a widely held belief is that *all grammars leak*—that it is not possible to specify a language completely by grammar rules.

In compiler construction, grammars have a similar role: they give rules for forming "words", such as integer constants, identifiers, and keywords. And they also give rules for combining words into expressions, statements, and programs. But the usefulness of grammars is much less controversial than in linguistics: grammars of programming languages don't leak, because the languages are *defined* by their grammars. This is possible because programming languages are artificial products, rather than results of natural evolution.

Defining a programming language is so easy that we can directly jump into doing it. Let us start with the grammar in Figure 2.1. It defines a language of **expressions** built by using the four arithmetic operations (addition, sub-

```
EAdd. Exp  ::= Exp  "+" Exp1 ;
ESub. Exp  ::= Exp  "-" Exp1 ;
EMul. Exp1 ::= Exp1 "*" Exp2 ;
EDiv. Exp1 ::= Exp1 "/" Exp2 ;
EInt. Exp2 ::= Integer ;

coercions Exp 2 ;
```

Figure 2.1: `Calc.cf`, a labelled BNF grammar for integer arithmetic.

traction, multiplication, division) as well as integer constants. You can copy this code into a file called `Calc.cf`. It will be the source of your first compiler component, which is a parser of integer arithmetic expressions.

The code in Figure 2.1 is written in the notation of BNFC, BNF Converter. It is a brand of the **BNF** notation, **Backus Naur Form**, named after the two inventors of this grammar format. BNF grammars are routinely used for the **specification of programming languages**, appearing in language manuals. The parser of a language must of course follow the grammar in order to be correct. If the grammar is written in the BNFC notation, such a correct parser can be automatically derived by the BNFC tool.

The code in Figure 2.1 should be easy to understand, at least roughly. It specifies that expressions (`Exp`) can be combined with the four operators +, -, *, and /, ultimately from integers (`Integer`). We will explain the details of the notation in a while, in particular the digit suffixes in `Exp1` and `Exp2`, as well as `coercions` and the labels such as `EAdd`. But we will first show how the code is used in BNFC.

2.2   Using BNFC

The first thing you have to do is to check that the BNFC tool is available. Assuming you are working in a Unix-style shell, type

```
bnfc
```

and you should get a message specifying the authors and license of BNFC and its usage options. If the command `bnfc` does not work, you can install the software from the BNFC homepage, which is linked from the book's web page. BNFC is available for Linux, Mac OS, and Windows, and there are several installation methods (such as Debian packages), from which you can choose the one most suitable for your platform and taste. Each platform also has Unix-style shells: Cygwin in Windows and Terminal in Mac OS.

Now, assuming you have BNFC installed, you can run it on the file `Calc.cf` in Figure 2.1.

```
bnfc -m Calc.cf
```

The system will respond by generating a bunch of files:

```
writing file AbsCalc.hs     # abstract syntax
writing file LexCalc.x      # lexer
writing file ParCalc.y      # parser
writing file DocCalc.tex    # language document
writing file SkelCalc.hs    # syntax-directed translation skeleton
writing file PrintCalc.hs   # pretty-printer
writing file TestCalc.hs    # top-level test program
writing file ErrM.hs        # monad for error handling
writing file Makefile       # Makefile
```

These files are different components of a compiler, which can be automatically generated from the BNF grammar. The suffix `.hs` tells that some of the files are for the Haskell programming language. We shall see later how other languages can be used instead. For instance, you can write

```
bnfc -m -java Calc.cf
```

to generate the components for Java. (Writing `java1.4` also works, but generates clumsier code that doesn't use Java's generics.)

Running BNFC for Haskell

One of the generated files is a `Makefile`, which specifies the commands for compiling the compiler. So let us do this as the next thing:

```
make
```

Again, this can fail at some point if you don't have the Haskell tools installed: the GHC Haskell compiler, the Happy parser generator, and the Alex lexer generator. You don't need to install them, if you aim to work in Java and not in Haskell, but let us first assume you do have GHC, Happy, and Alex. Then your run of `make` will successfully terminate with the message

```
Linking TestCalc ...
```

`TestCalc` is an executable program for testing the parser defined by `Calc.cf`. So let us try it out:

```
echo "5 + 6 * 7" | ./TestCalc
```

Notice that `TestCalc` reads Unix standard input; the easiest thing to provide the parsable expression is thus by a pipe from the `echo` command. Then, the response of `TestCalc` is the following:

```
Parse Successful!

[Abstract Syntax]
EAdd (EInt 5) (EMul (EInt 6) (EInt 7))

[Linearized tree]
5 + 6 * 7
```

It first says that it has succeeded to parse the input, then shows an **abstract syntax tree**, which is the result of parsing and gives the tree structure of the expression. Finally, it displays the **linearization**, which is the string obtained by using the grammar in the direction opposite to parsing. This string can be different from the input string, for instance, if the input has unnecessary parentheses.

Input can also be read from a file. The standard input method for this is

```
./TestCalc < FILE_with_an_expression
```

But the test program also allows a file name argument,

```
./TestCalc FILE_with_an_expression
```

Running BNFC for Java

If you use Java rather than Haskell, you will run BNFC with the `-java` option,

```
bnfc -m -java Calc.cf
```

You see that some more files are generated then:

```
Calc/Absyn/Exp.java          # abstract syntax
Calc/Absyn/EAdd.java
Calc/Absyn/ESub.java
Calc/Absyn/EMul.java
Calc/Absyn/EDiv.java
Calc/Absyn/EInt.java
Calc/PrettyPrinter.java      # pretty-printer
Calc/VisitSkel.java          # syntax-directed translation skeleton
Calc/ComposVisitor.java      # utilities for syntax-dir. transl
Calc/AbstractVisitor.java
Calc/FoldVisitor.java
```

```
Calc/AllVisitor.java
Calc/Test.java              # top-level test file
Calc/Yylex                  # lexer
Calc/Calc.cup               # parser
Calc.tex                    # language document
Makefile                    # Makefile
```

There are no Haskell files any more, but files for Java, its parser tool Cup, and its lexer tool JLex. The Makefile works exactly like in the case of Haskell:

```
make
```

Well... if you have done exactly as shown above, you will probably fail with the message

```
java  JLex.Main Calc/Yylex
Exception in thread "main" java.lang.NoClassDefFoundError: JLex/Main
make: *** [Calc/Yylex.java] Error 1
```

This problem is typical in Java when using libraries that reside in unusual places, which often happens with user-installed libraries like Cup and JLex. Fortunately there is an easy solution: you just have to define the **class path** that Java uses for finding libraries. On my Ubuntu Linux laptop, the following shell command does the job:

```
export CLASSPATH=.:/usr/local/java/Cup:/usr/local/java
```

Now I will get a better result with make. Then I can run the parser test in almost the same way as with the version compiled with Haskell:

```
echo "5 + 6 * 7" | java Calc/Test

Parse Successful!

[Abstract Syntax]
(EAdd (EInt 5) (EMul (EInt 6) (EInt 7)))

[Linearized Tree]
5 + 6 * 7
```

To summarize, these are the two most important facts about BNFC:

1. We can use a BNF grammar to generate several compiler components.

2. The components can be generated in different languages from the same BNF source.

2.3 Rules, categories, and trees

A BNFC source file is a sequence of **rules**, where most rules have the format

> *Label . Category* ::= *Production* ;

The *Label* and *Category* are **identifiers** (without quotes). The *Production* is
a sequence of two kinds of items:

- identifiers, called **nonterminals**

- **string literals** (strings in double quotes), called **terminals**

The rule has the following semantics:

- A **tree** of type *Category* can be built with *Label* as the topmost node,
  from any sequence specified by the production, whose nonterminals give
  the subtrees of the tree built.

Types of trees are the **categories** of the grammar, that is, the different kinds of
objects that can be built (expressions, statements, programs,. . .). Tree labels
are the **constructors** of those categories. The constructors appear as nodes
of abstract syntax trees. Thus we saw above that the string

```
5 + 6 * 7
```

was compiled into a tree displayed as follows:

```
EAdd (EInt 5) (EMul (EInt 6) (EInt 7))
```

You may also notice that it is *exactly* the notation Haskell programmers use for
specifying a certain kind of trees: expressions built by function applications.
But it is also a handy (machine-readable!) notation for the "real" tree

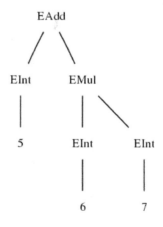

2.4   Precedence levels

How does BNFC know that multiplication is performed before addition, that is, why the `EMul` node is below the `EAdd` node? Another way for analysing the expression `5 + 6 * 7` could be

```
EMul (EAdd (EInt 5) (EInt 6)) (EInt 7)
```

The reason we don't give this analysis is that multiplication expressions have a **higher precedence**. In BNFC, **precedence levels** are the digits attached to category symbols. Thus `Exp1` has precedence level 1, `Exp2` has precedence level 2, etc. The nonterminal `Exp` without a digit is defined to mean the same as `Exp0`.

The rule

```
EAdd. Exp  ::= Exp  "+" Exp1 ;
```

can be read as saying:

> `EAdd` forms an expression of level 0 from an expression of level 0 on the left of + and of level 1 on the right.

Likewise, the rule

```
EMul. Exp1 ::= Exp1 "*" Exp2 ;
```

says: `EMul` form an expression of level 1 from an expression of level 1 on the left of * and of level 2 on the right.

The semantics of precedence levels consists of three principles:

1. All precedence variants of a nonterminal denote the same type in the abstract syntax. Thus 2, 2 + 2, and 2 * 2 are all of type `Exp`.

2. An expression of higher level can always be used on lower levels as well. This is what makes 2 + 3 correct: integer literals have level 2 (Figure 2.1), but are here used on level 0 on the left and on level 1 on the right.

3. An expression of any level can be lifted to the highest level by putting it in parentheses. Thus (5 + 6) is an expression of level 2

What is the highest level? This is specified in the grammar by using a `coercions` statement. For instance, `coercions Exp 2` says that 2 is the highest level for `Exp`. It is actually a shorthand for the following "ordinary" BNF rules:

```
_. Exp0 ::= Exp1 ;
_. Exp1 ::= Exp2 ;
_. Exp2 ::= "(" Exp0 ")" ;
```

These rules are called **coercions**, since they just coerce expressions from one category to another, without doing anything—that is, without creating new nodes in the abstract syntax tree. The underscore _ in front of these rules is a **dummy label**, which indicates that no constructor is added.

2.5   Abstract and concrete syntax

Abstract syntax trees are the hub of a modern compiler: they are the target of the parser and the place where most compilation phases happen, including type checking and code generation.

Abstract syntax is purely about the structure of expressions: what are their immediate parts and the parts of those parts? Abstract syntax thus ignore questions like what the parts look like, or even what order they appear in. From an abstract syntax point of view, all of the following expressions are the same:

2 + 3	Java, C (infix)
(+ 2 3)	Lisp (prefix)
(2 3 +)	postfix
bipush 2	JVM (postfix)
bipush 3	
iadd	
the sum of 2 and 3	English (prefix/mixfix)
2:n ja 3:n summa	Finnish (postfix/mixfix)

In fact, the simplest way to build a compiler is the following:

1. Parse the source language expression, e.g. 2 + 3.

2. Obtain an abstract syntax tree, EAdd (EInt 2) (EInt 3).

3. Linearize the tree to another format, bipush 2 bipush 3 iadd.

In practice, compilers don't quite work in this simple way. The main reason is that the tree obtained in parsing may have to be converted to another tree before code generation. For instance, type annotations may have to be added to an arithmetic expression tree in order to select the proper JVM instructions.

The BNF grammar specifies the abstract syntax of a language. But it simultaneously specifies its **concrete syntax** as well. The concrete syntax gives more detail than the abstract syntax: it says what the expression parts look like and in what order they appear. One way to spell out the distinction is by trying to separate these aspects in a BNF rule. Take, for instance, the rule for addition expressions:

```
EAdd. Exp0 ::= Exp0 "+" Exp1
```

The purely abstract syntax part of this rule is

```
EAdd. Exp   ::= Exp      Exp
```

which hides the actual symbol used for addition (and thereby the place where it appears). It also hides the precedence levels, since they don't imply any differences in the abstract syntax trees.

In brief, the abstract syntax is extracted from a BNF grammar as follows:

1. Remove all terminals.

2. Remove all precedence numbers.

3. Remove all `coercions` rules.

If this is performed with `Calc.cf` (Figure 2.1), the following rules remain:

```
EAdd. Exp ::= Exp Exp ;
ESub. Exp ::= Exp Exp ;
EMul. Exp ::= Exp Exp ;
EDiv. Exp ::= Exp Exp ;
EInt. Exp ::= Integer ;
```

This is a kind of a "skeleton" of a grammar, which could be filled with terminals, precedence numbers, and coercions in different ways to obtain new languages with the same abstract syntax. For instance, JVM assembler could be constructed as follows:

```
EAdd. Exp ::= Exp Exp "iadd" ;
ESub. Exp ::= Exp Exp "isub" ;
EMul. Exp ::= Exp Exp "imul" ;
EDiv. Exp ::= Exp Exp "idiv" ;
EInt. Exp ::= "bipush" Integer ;
```

Now it is easy to see that arithmetic expressions could be compiled to JVM by just combining parsing with `Calc.cf` and linearization with this alternative grammar.

Another way to see the distinction between abstract and concrete syntax is by means of the different kinds of trees they involve. What we have called **abstract syntax trees** have a simple structure:

- their nodes and leaves are constructors (i.e. labels of BNF rules).

In contrast, **concrete syntax trees**, also called **parse trees**, look different:

- their nodes are category symbols (i.e. nonterminals)

- their leaves are tokens (i.e. terminals)

Here are the parse tree and the abstract syntax tree for the expression 5 + 6 * 7 as analysed by `Calc.cf`:

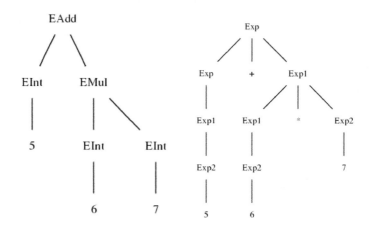

A parse tree is an accurate encoding of the sequence of BNF rules applied, and hence it shows all coercions between precedence levels and all tokens in the input string.

2.6   Abstract syntax in Haskell

The purpose of abstract syntax is to provide a suitable platform for further processing in a compiler. Concrete syntax details such as precedences and the shapes of the terminals are then irrelevant: it would just complicate the matters, and also weaken the portability of compiler back-end components to other languages.

Haskell is the language with the most straightforward representations of abstract syntax, so let us start with it. Java will be covered in the next section. And we will return to the details of abstract syntax programming later, when discussing later compiler phases. We hope the Haskell code we show is readable by non-Haskellers as well—it is much simpler than the Java code for the same purpose.

When generating Haskell code, BNFC represents the abstract syntax by **algebraic datatypes**. For every category in the grammar, a **data** definition is thus produced. The `Exp` category of `Calc` generates the following definition:

```
data Exp =
   EAdd Exp Exp
 | ESub Exp Exp
 | EMul Exp Exp
 | EDiv Exp Exp
 | EInt Integer
```

The main programming method in most components of the compiler is **syntax-directed translation**, i.e. **structural recursion on abstract syntax trees**. In Haskell, this is performed conveniently by using **pattern matching**. The following code is, in fact, the complete implementation of a calculator, which evaluates arithmetic expressions into integer values; thus it is an interpreter for this tiny language:

```
module Interpreter where

import AbsCalc

eval :: Exp -> Integer
eval x = case x of
  EAdd exp1 exp2  -> eval exp1 + eval exp2
  ESub exp1 exp2  -> eval exp1 - eval exp2
  EMul exp1 exp2  -> eval exp1 * eval exp2
  EDiv exp1 exp2  -> eval exp1 'div' eval exp2
  EInt n  -> n
```

Thus we can now turn our parser into an interpreter! We do this by modifying the generated file `TestCalc.hs`: instead of showing the syntax tree, we let it show the value from interpretation:

```
module Main where

import LexCalc
import ParCalc
import AbsCalc
import Interpreter
import ErrM

main = do
  interact calc
  putStrLn ""

calc s = let Ok e = pExp (myLexer s)
         in show (interpret e)
```

This, in a nutshell, is how you can build any compiler on top of BNFC:

1. Write a grammar and convert it into parser and other modules.

2. Write some code that manipulates syntax trees in a desired way.

3. Let the main file show the results of syntax tree manipulation.

If your `Main` module is in a file named `Calculator`, you can compile it with GHC as follows:

```
ghc --make Calculator.hs
```

Then you can run it on command-line input:

```
echo "1 + 2 * 3" | ./Calculator
7
```

Now, let's do the same thing in Java.

2.7   Abstract syntax in Java

Java has no notation for algebraic datatypes. But such types can be encoded by using the class system of Java:

- For each category in the grammar, an abstract base class.

- For each constructor of the category, a class extending the base class.

This means quite a few files, which are for the sake of clarity put to a separate directory `Absyn`. In the case of `Calc.cf`, we have the files

```
Calc/Absyn/EAdd.java
Calc/Absyn/EDiv.java
Calc/Absyn/EInt.java
Calc/Absyn/EMul.java
Calc/Absyn/ESub.java
Calc/Absyn/Exp.java
```

This is what the classes look like; we ignore some of the code in them now and only show the parts crucial for abstract syntax representation:

- `Integer`, **integer literals**: sequence of digits, e.g. `123445425425436`;

- `Double`, **float literals**: two sequences of digits with a decimal point in between, possibly with an exponent after, e.g. `7.098e-7`;

- `String`, **string literals**: any characters between double quotes, e.g. `"hello world"`, with a backslash (\) escaping a quote and a backslash;

- `Char`, **character literals**: any character between single quotes, e.g. `'x'` and `'7'`;

- `Ident`, **identifiers**: a letter (`A..Za..z`) followed by letters, digits, and characters _ or ', e.g. `r2_out'`

The precise definitions of these types are given in the LBNF report, Appendix A. Notice that the integer and floating point literals do not contain negative numbers; negation is usually defined in a grammar rule as a prefix operator working for expressions other than literals, too.

The predefined token types are often sufficient for language implementations, especially for new languages, which can be designed to follow the BNFC rules for convenience. But BNFC also allows the definition of new token types. These definitions are written by using **regular expressions**. For instance, one can define a special type of upper-case identifiers as follows:

```
token UIdent (upper (letter | digit | '_')*) ;
```

This defines `UIdent` as a **token type**, which contains strings starting with an upper-case letter and continuing with a (possibly empty) sequence of letters, digits, and underscores.

The following table gives the main regular expressions available in BNFC.

name	notation	explanation
symbol	`'a'`	the character `a`
sequence	$A\ B$	A followed by B
union	$A \mid B$	A or B
closure	$A*$	any number of A's (possibly 0)
empty	`eps`	the empty string
character	`char`	any character (ASCII 0..255)
letter	`letter`	any letter (`A..Za..z`)
upper-case letter	`upper`	any upper-case letter (`A..Z`)
lower-case letter	`lower`	any lower-case letter (`a..z`)
digit	`digit`	any digit (`0..9`)
option	$A?$	optional A
difference	$A - B$	A which is not B

We will return to the semantics and implementation of regular expressions in Chapter 3.

BNFC can be forced to remember the **position of a token**. This is useful when, for instance, error messages at later compilation phases make reference to the source code. The notation for token types remembering the position is

```
position token CIdent (letter | (letter | digit | '_')*) ;
```

When BNFC is run, bare `token` types are encoded as types of strings. For instance, the standard `Ident` type is in Haskell represented as

```
newtype Ident = Ident String
```

Position token types add to this a pair of integers indicating the line and the column in the input:

```
newtype CIdent = CIdent (String, (Int,Int))
```

In addition to tokens, **comments** are a language feature treated in the lexer. They are parts of source code that the compiler ignores. BNFC permits the definition of two kinds of comments:

- single-line comments, which run from a start token till the end of the line;

- arbitrary-length comments, which run from a start token till a closing token.

This is, for instance, how comments of C are defined:

```
comment "//" ;
comment "/*" "*/" ;
```

Thus single-line comments need one token, the start token, whereas arbitrary-length comments need the opening and the closing token.

Since comments are resolved by the lexer, they are processed by using a finite automaton. Therefore nested comments are not possible. A more thorough explanation of this will be given in next chapter.

2.10 Working out a grammar

We conclude this section by working out a grammar for a small C-like programming language. This language is the same as targeted by the Assignments 2 to 4 at the end of this book, called **CPP**. Assignment 1 targets a larger language, for which this smaller language is a good starting point. The discussion below goes through the language constructs top-down, i.e. from the largest to the smallest, and builds the appropriate rules at each stage.

- *A program is a sequence of definitions.*

This suggests the following BNFC rules:

```
PDefs.     Program ::= [Def] ;

terminator Def "" ;
```

- *A program may contain comments, which are ignored by the parser. Comments can start with the token // and extend to the end of the line. They can also start with /* and extend to the next */.*

This means C-like comments, which are specified as follows:

```
comment "//" ;
comment "/*" "*/" ;
```

- *A function definition has a type, a name, an argument list, and a body. An argument list is a comma-separated list of argument declarations enclosed in parentheses (and). A function body is a list of statements enclosed in curly brackets { and } . For example:*

```
      int foo(double x, int y)
      {
        return y + 9 ;
      }
```

We decide to specify all parts of a function definition in one rule, in addition to which we specify the form of argument and statement lists:

```
DFun.      Def      ::= Type Id "(" [Arg] ")" "{" [Stm] "}" ;
separator  Arg "," ;
terminator Stm "" ;
```

- *An argument declaration has a type and an identifier.*

```
ADecl.   Arg    ::= Type Id ;
```

- *Any expression followed by a semicolon ; can be used as a statement.*

```
SExp.    Stm    ::= Exp ";" ;
```

- *Any declaration followed by a semicolon ; can be used as a statement. Declarations have one of the following formats:*
  - *a type and one variable (as in function parameter lists),*

```
           int i ;
 − a type and many variables,
           int i, j ;
 − a type and one initialized variable,
           int i = 6 ;
```

Now, we could reuse the function argument declarations `Arg` as one kind of statements. But we choose the simpler solution of restating the rule for one-variable declarations.

```
SDecl.   Stm    ::= Type Id ";" ;
SDecls.  Stm    ::= Type Id "," [Id] ";" ;
SInit.   Stm    ::= Type Id "=" Exp ";" ;
```

- *Statements also include*
  - *Statements returning an expression,*
    ```
    return i + 9 ;
    ```
  - *While loops, with an expression in parentheses followed by a statement,*
    ```
    while (i < 10) ++i ;
    ```
  - *Conditionals:* *if with an expression in parentheses followed by a statement,* *else,* *and another statement,*
    ```
    if (x > 0) return x ; else return y ;
    ```
  - *Blocks: any list of statements (including the empty list) between curly brackets. For instance,*
    ```
    {
      int i = 2 ;
      {
      }
      i++ ;
    }
    ```

The statement specifications give rise to the following BNF rules:

```
SReturn. Stm    ::= "return" Exp ";" ;
SWhile.  Stm    ::= "while" "(" Exp ")" Stm ;
SBlock.  Stm    ::= "{" [Stm] "}" ;
SIfElse. Stm    ::= "if" "(" Exp ")" Stm "else" Stm ;
```

- *Expressions are specified with the following table that gives their precedence levels. Infix operators are assumed to be left-associative, except assignments, which are right-associative. The arguments in a function call can be expressions of any level. Otherwise, the subexpressions are assumed to be one precedence level above the main expression.*

level	expression forms	explanation
15	literal	literal (integer, float, string, boolean)
15	identifier	variable
15	f(e,...,e)	function call
14	v++, v--	post-increment, post-decrement
13	++v, --v	pre-increment, pre-decrement
13	-e	numeric negation
12	e*e, e/e	multiplication, division
11	e+e, e-e	addition, subtraction
9	e<e, e>e, e>=e, e<=e	comparison
8	e==e, e!=e	(in)equality
4	e&&e	conjunction
3	e||e	disjunction
2	v=e	assignment

The table is straightforward to translate to a set of BNFC rules. On the level of literals, integers and floats ("doubles") are provided by BNFC, whereas the boolean literals true and false are defined by special rules.

```
EInt.     Exp15  ::= Integer ;
EDouble.  Exp15  ::= Double ;
EString.  Exp15  ::= String ;
ETrue.    Exp15  ::= "true" ;
EFalse.   Exp15  ::= "false" ;
EId.      Exp15  ::= Id ;

ECall.    Exp15  ::= Id "(" [Exp] ")" ;

EPIncr.   Exp14  ::= Exp15 "++" ;
EPDecr.   Exp14  ::= Exp15 "--" ;

EIncr.    Exp13  ::= "++" Exp14 ;
EDecr.    Exp13  ::= "--" Exp14 ;
ENeg.     Exp13  ::= "-" Exp14 ;

EMul.     Exp12  ::= Exp12 "*"  Exp13 ;
EDiv.     Exp12  ::= Exp12 "/"  Exp13 ;
EAdd.     Exp11  ::= Exp11 "+"  Exp12 ;
ESub.     Exp11  ::= Exp11 "-"  Exp12 ;
ELt.      Exp9   ::= Exp9  "<"  Exp10 ;
EGt.      Exp9   ::= Exp9  ">"  Exp10 ;
ELEq.     Exp9   ::= Exp9  "<=" Exp10 ;
EGEq.     Exp9   ::= Exp9  ">=" Exp10 ;
```

```
EEq.     Exp8    ::= Exp8  "==" Exp9 ;
ENEq.    Exp8    ::= Exp8  "!=" Exp9 ;
EAnd.    Exp4    ::= Exp4  "&&" Exp5 ;
EOr.     Exp3    ::= Exp3  "||" Exp4 ;
EAss.    Exp2    ::= Exp3 "=" Exp2 ;
```

Finally, we need a `coercions` rule to specify the highest precedence level, and a rule to form function argument lists.

```
coercions Exp 15 ;
separator Exp "," ;
```

- *The available types are* bool, double, int, string, *and* void.

```
Tbool.   Type ::= "bool" ;
Tdouble. Type ::= "double" ;
Tint.    Type ::= "int" ;
Tstring. Type ::= "string" ;
Tvoid.   Type ::= "void" ;
```

- *An identifier is a letter followed by a list of letters, digits, and underscores.*

Here we cannot use the built-in `Ident` type of BNFC, because apostrophes (') are not permitted! But we can define our identifiers easily by a regular expression:

```
token Id (letter (letter | digit | '_')*) ;
```

Alternatively, we could write

```
position token Id (letter (letter | digit | '_')*) ;
```

to remember the source code positions of identifiers.

The reader is advised to copy all the rules of this section into a file and try this out in BNFC, with various programs as input. The grammar is also available on the book web page.

Chapter 3

Lexing and Parsing*

This is an optional theory chapter, which gives deeper understanding of the things worked through in the previous chapter. It explains the concepts of regular expressions and finite automata, context-free grammars and parsing algorithms, and the limits of each of these methods. For instance, we will show why automata may explode in size, why parentheses cannot be matched by finite automata, and why context-free grammars cannot alone specify the well-formedness of programs. We will also look at how the usual parsing algorithms work, to understand what **conflicts** are and how to avoid them.

3.1 The theory of formal languages

BNFC saves a lot of work in compiler writing by generating the code needed for the lexer and the parser. The saving is by an order of magnitude, compared with hand-written code in the targeted tools (see Section 8.7). The code generated by BNFC is processed by other tools, which in turn generate code in some host language—Haskell, Java, or C. Let us call the lexer tool (Alex, JLex, Flex) just **Lex** and the parser tool (Happy, Cup, Bison) just **Yacc**, by references to the first such tools created for C in the 1970's. These tools stand for another order of magnitude of saving, compared to writing host language code by hand.

The generation of Lex and Yacc from a BNFC file is rather straightforward. The next step is much more involved. In a nutshell,

- **Lex** code is **regular expressions**, converted to **finite automata**.

- **Yacc** code is **context-free grammars**, converted to **LALR(1) parsers**.

Regular expressions and context-free grammars, as well as their compilation to automata and parsers, originate in the mathematical theory of **formal languages**. A formal language is, mathematically, just any set of **sequences of**

symbols, where **symbols** are just elements from any finite set, such as the 128 7-bit ASCII characters. Programming languages are examples of formal languages. They are rather complex in comparison to the examples usually studied in the theory; but the good news is that their complexity is mostly due to repetitions of simple well-known patterns.

3.2 Regular languages and finite automata

A **regular language** is, like any formal language, a set of **strings**, i.e. sequences of **symbols**, from a finite set of symbols called the **alphabet**. Only some formal languages are regular; in fact, regular languages are exactly those that can be defined by **regular expressions**, which we already saw in Section 2.9. We don't even need all the expressions, but just five of them; the other ones are convenient shorthands. They are shown in the following table, together with the corresponding regular language in set-theoretic notation:

expression	language
'a'	$\{a\}$
AB	$\{ab \mid a \in [\![A]\!], b \in [\![B]\!]\}$
$A \mid B$	$[\![A]\!] \cup [\![B]\!]$
$A*$	$\{a_1 a_2 \ldots a_n \mid a_i \in [\![A]\!], n \geq 0\}$
eps	$\{\epsilon\}$ (empty string)

The table uses the notation $[\![A]\!]$ for the set corresponding to the expression A. This notation is common in computer science to specify the **semantics** of a language, in terms of the **denotations** of expressions.

When does a string belong to a regular language? A straightforward answer would be to write a program that *interprets* the sets, e.g. in Haskell by using list comprehensions instead of the set brackets. This implementation, however, would be very inefficient. The usual way to go is to *compile* regular expressions to **finite automata**. Finite automata are graphs that allow traversing their input strings symbol by symbol. For example, the following automaton recognizes a string that is either an integer literal or an identifier or a string literal.

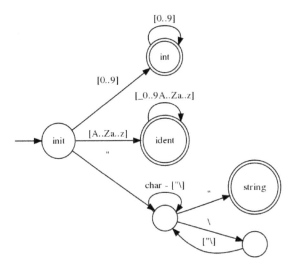

The corresponding regular expression is

```
   digit digit*
 | letter ('_' | letter | digit)*
 | '"' (char - ('\' | '"') | '\' ('\' | '"'))* '"'
```

The automaton can be used for the **recognition of tokens**. In this case, a recognized token is either a decimal integer, an identifier, or a string literal. The recognition starts from the **initial state**, that is, the node marked "init". It goes to the next **state** depending on the first character. If it is a digit 0...9, the state is the one marked "int". With more digits, the recognition loops back to this state. The state is marked with a double circle, which means it is a **final state**, also known as an **accepting state**. The other accepting states are "ident" and "string". But on the way to "string", there are non-accepting states: the one before a second quote is read, and the one after an escape (backslash) is read.

The automaton above is **deterministic**, which means that at any state, any input symbol has at most one **transition**, that is, at most one way to go to a next state. If a symbol with no transition is encountered, the string is not accepted. For instance, **a&b** would not be an accepted string in the above automaton; nor is it covered by the regular expression.

An automaton can also be **nondeterministic**, which means that some symbols may have many transitions. An example is the following automaton, with the corresponding regular expression that recognizes the language $\{ab, ac\}$:

```
   a b | a c
```

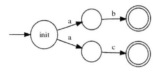

Now, this automaton and indeed the expression might look like a stupid thing to write anyway: wouldn't it be much smarter to factor out the a and write simply as follows?

    a (b | c)

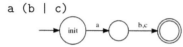

The answer is *no*, both surprisingly and in a way typical to compiler construction. The reason is that one should not try to optimize automata by hand—one should let a compiler do that automatically and much more reliably! Generating a non-deterministic automaton is the standard first step of compiling regular expressions. After that, deterministic and, indeed, minimal automata can be obtained as optimizations.

Just to give an idea of how tedious it can be to create deterministic automata by hand, think about compiling an English dictionary into an automaton. It may start as follows:

    a able about account acid across act addition adjustment

It would be a real pain to write a bracketed expression in the style of a (c | b), and much nicer to just put |'s between the words and let the compiler do the rest!

Exercise 3-0. We showed an automaton for integers, identifiers, and strings. Complete it into an automaton that recognizes any *sequence* of such tokens, with any number of spaces in between. When are spaces obligatory, to keep the automaton deterministic?

Exercise 3-1. Write a regular expression for comments of the form /* ... */. Construct a nondeterministic and a deterministic automaton for this kind of comments.

3.3   The compilation of regular expressions

The standard compilation of regular expressions has the following steps:

1. **NFA generation**: convert the expression into a **non-deterministic finite automaton, NFA**.

2. **Determination**: convert the NFA into a **deterministic finite automaton, DFA**.

3. **Minimization**: minimize the size of the deterministic automaton.

As usual in compilers, each of these phases is simple in itself, but trying to do them all at once would be too complicated.

Step 1. NFA generation

Assuming we have an expression written by just the five basic operators, we can build an NFA which has exactly one initial state and exactly one final state. The "exactly one" condition is crucial to make it easy to combine the automata for sequences, unions, and closures. The easiest way to guarantee this is to use **epsilon transitions**, that is, transitions that consume no input. They are marked with the symbol ϵ in the graphs. They of course increase nondeterminism, but can be eliminated later.

- **Symbol**. The expression a is compiled to

- **Sequence**. The expression $A\ B$ is compiled by combining the automata for A and B (drawn with dashed figures with one initial and one final state) as follows:

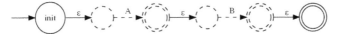

- **Union**. The expression $A \mid B$ is compiled as follows:

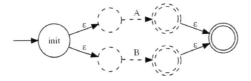

- **Closure**. The expression $A*$ is compiled as follows:

- **Empty**. The expression eps is compiled to

NFA generation is an example of **syntax-directed translation**, and could be recommended as an extra assignment for everyone! What is needed is a parser and abstract syntax for regular expressions (by BNFC), and a suitable code representation for automata. From this representation, one could also generate visualizations using e.g. the Graphviz software (as we did when preparing this book). Here is an example of an automaton and its Graphviz code:

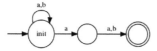

```
digraph {
  rankdir = LR ;
  start [label = "",      shape = "plaintext"]
  init  [label = "init",  shape = "circle"] ;
  a     [label = "",      shape = "circle"] ;
  end   [label = "",      shape = "doublecircle"] ;
  start -> init ;
  init  -> init [label = "a,b"] ;
  init  -> a    [label = "a"] ;
  a     -> end  [label = "a,b"] ;
}
```

The intermediate abstract representation should encode the mathematical definition of automata:

> *Definition.* A **finite automaton** is a 5-tuple $\langle \Sigma, S, F, i, t \rangle$ where
>
> - Σ is a finite set of symbols (the **alphabet**)
> - S is a finite set of **states**
> - $F \subset S$ (the **final states**)
> - $i \in S$ (the **initial state**)
> - $t : S \times \Sigma \to \mathcal{P}(S)$ (the **transition function**)
>
> An automaton is **deterministic**, if $t(s, a)$ is a singleton for all $s \in S, a \in \Sigma$. Otherwise, it is **nondeterministic**, and then moreover the transition function is generalized to $t : S \times \Sigma \cup \{\epsilon\} \to \mathcal{P}(S)$ (with **epsilon transitions**).

Step 2. Determination

One of the most powerful and amazing properties of finite automata is that they can always be made deterministic by a fairly simple procedure. The procedure is called the **subset construction**. In brief: for every state s and symbol a

in the automaton, form a new state $\sigma(s, a)$ that "gathers" all those states to which there is a transition from s by a. More precisely:

- $\sigma(s, a)$ is the set of those states s_i to which one can arrive from s by consuming just the symbol a. This includes of course the states to which the path contains epsilon transitions.

- The transitions from $\sigma(s, a) = \{s_1, \ldots, s_n\}$ for a symbol b are all the transitions with b from any s_i. (When this is specified, the subset construction must of course be iterated to build $\sigma(\sigma(s, a), b)$.)

- The state $\sigma(s, a) = \{s_1, \ldots, s_n\}$ is final if any of s_i is final.

Let us give a complete example. Starting with the "awful" expression

```
a b | a c
```

the NFA generation of Step 1 creates the monstrous automaton

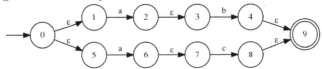

From this, the subset construction gives

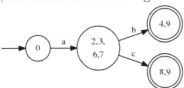

How does this come out? First we look at the possible transitions with the symbol a from state 0. Because of epsilon transitions, there are no less than four possible states, which we collect to the state named $\{2,3,6,7\}$. From this state, b can lead to 4 and 9, because there is a b-transition from 3 to 4 and an epsilon transition from 4 to 9. Similarly, c can lead to 8 and 9.

The resulting automaton is deterministic but not yet minimal. Therefore we perform one more optimization.

Step 3. Minimization

Determination may left the automaton with superfluous states. This means that there are states without any **distinguishing strings**. A distinguishing string for states s and u is a sequence x of symbols that ends up in an accepting state when starting from s and in a non-accepting state when starting from u.

For example, in the previous deterministic automaton, the states 0 and $\{2,3,6,7\}$ are distinguished by the string ab. When starting from 0, it leads to the final state $\{4,9\}$. When starting from $\{2,3,6,7\}$, there are no transitions marked for **a**, which means that any string starting with **a** ends up in a **dead state** which is non-accepting.

But the states $\{4,9\}$ and $\{8,9\}$ are not distinguished by any string. The only string that ends to a final state is the empty string, from both of them. The minimization can thus merge these states, and we get the final, optimized automaton

The algorithm for minimization is a bit more complicated than for determination. We omit its details here.

Exercise 3-2.+ Write a compiler from regular expressions to NFA's, covering the minimal set (symbol, sequence, union, closure, empty) and the notation used in the presentation above. You can use BNFC and define a suitable token type for symbols (Section 2.9). As for the precedences, closure should bind stronger than sequence, sequence stronger than union. The automata and the compiler can be expressed in a mathematical notation and pseudocode. For instance, the definition of automata for one-symbol expressions suggests

$$compile(ESymbol\ a) = \langle \Sigma, \{0,1\}, \{1\}, 0, \{((0,a),1)\} \rangle$$

You can also write an actual compiler as a back-end to the parser. If you are really ambitious, you can generate Graphviz code to show all the bubbles!

3.4   Properties of regular languages

There is a whole branch of discrete mathematics dealing with regular languages and finite automata. A part of the research has to do with **closure properties**. For instance, regular languages are closed under **complement**, i.e. if L is a regular language, then also $-L$, is one: the set of all those strings of the alphabet that do not belong to L.

We said that the five operators compiled in the previous section were sufficient to define all regular languages. Other operators can be defined in terms of them; for instance, the non-empty closure A^+ is simply AA^*. The negation operator $-A$ is more complicated to define; in fact, the simplest way to see that it exists is to recall that regular languages are closed under negation.

But how do we *know* that regular languages are closed under negation? The simplest way to do this is to construct an automaton: assume that we have a DFA corresponding to A. Then the automaton for $-A$ is obtained by inverting the status of each accepting state to non-accepting and vice-versa! This requires a version of the DFA where all symbols have transitions from every state; this can always be guaranteed by adding a dedicated dead state as a goal for those symbols that are impossible to continue with.

The reasoning above relies on the **correspondence theorem** saying that the following three are equivalent, convertible to each other: regular languages, regular expressions, finite automata. The determination algorithm moreover proves that there is always a *deterministic* automaton. The closure property for regular languages and expressions follows. (The theorem is due to Stephen Kleene, the father of regular expressions and automata. After him, the closure construction A* is also known as the **Kleene star**.)

Another interesting property is inherent in the subset construction: the size of a DFA can be exponential in the size of the NFA (and therefore of the expression). The subset construction shows a potential for this, because there could in principle be a different state in the DFA for *every* subset of the NFA, and the number of subsets of an n-element set is 2^n.

A concrete example of the **size explosion of automata** is a language of strings of a's and b's, where the nth element *from the end* is an a. Consider this in the case $n=2$. The regular expression and NFA are easy:

(a|b)* a (a|b)

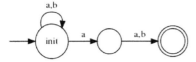

But how on earth can we make this deterministic? How can we know, when reading a string, *which* a is the second-last element so that we can stop looping?

It is possible to solve this problem by the subset construction, which is left as an exercise. But there is also an elegant direct construction, which I learned from a student many years ago. The idea is that the *state* must "remember" the last two symbols that have been read. Thus the states can be named aa, ab, ba, and bb. The states aa and ab are accepting, because they have a as the second-last symbol; the other two are not accepting. Now, for any more symbols encountered, one can "forget" the previous second-last symbol and go to the next state accordingly. For instance, if you are in ab, then a leads to ba and b leads to bb. The complete automaton is here:

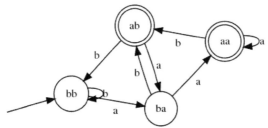

Notice that the initial state is bb, because a string must have at least two symbols in order to be accepted.

With a similar reasoning, it is easy to see that a DFA for a as the third-last symbol must have at least 8 states, for fourth-last 16, and so on. Unfortunately, the exponential blow-up of automata is not only a theoretical construct, but often happens in practice and can come as a surprise to those who build lexers by using regular expressions.

The third property of finite-state automata we want to address is, well, their finiteness. Remember from the definition that an automaton has a *finite* set of states. This fact can be used for proving that an automaton cannot match parentheses, i.e. guarantee that a string has as many left and right parentheses.

The argument uses, in the way typical of formal language theory, a's and b's to stand for left and right parentheses, respectively. The language we want to define is

$$\{a^n b^n | n = 0, 1, 2 \ldots\}$$

Now assume that the automaton is in state s_n after having read n a's and starting to read b's. This state must be different for every n, which means that there must be infinitely many states. For if we had $s_m = s_n$ for some $m \neq n$, then the automaton would recognize the expressions $a^n b^m$ and $a^m b^n$, which are not in the language! The automaton would look as follows:

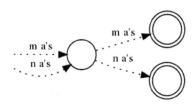

Matching parentheses is usually treated in parsers, which use BNF grammars; for the language in question, we can easily write the grammar

```
S ::= ;
S ::= "a" S "b" ;
```

and process it in parser tools. But there is a related construct that one might want to try to treat in a lexer: **nested comments**. The case in point is code of the form

```
a /* b /* c */ d */ e
```

One might expect the code after the removal of comments to be

```
a                        e
```

But actually it is, at least with standard compilers,

    a   d */ e

The reason is that the lexer is implemented by using a finite automaton, which cannot count the number of matching parentheses—in this case comment delimiters.

Exercise 3-3. Consider the simple NFA for the expression (a|b)* a (a|b) discussed in the text. Make it into a DFA by using the subset construction. Is the result different from the DFA constructed by informal reasoning?

Exercise 3-4. Test the explosion of automata in standard Lex-like tools by compiling regular expressions similar to the previous exercise but with a as the 10th-last or the 20th-last symbol. Do this by measuring the size of the generated code in Haskell (Alex), Java (JLex), or C (Flex).

3.5   Context-free grammars and parsing

A **context-free grammar** is the same as a **BNF grammar**, consisting of rules of the form

$$C ::= t_1 \ldots t_n$$

where each t_i is a terminal or a nonterminal. We used this format extensively in Chapter 2 together with labels for building abstract syntax trees. But for most discussion of parsing properties we can ignore the labels.

All regular languages can in fact also be defined by context-free grammars. The inverse does not hold, as proved by matching parentheses. The extra expressive power comes with a price: context-free parsing can be more complex than recognition with automata. It is easy to see that recognition with a finite automaton is *linear* in the length of the string ($O(n)$). But for context-free grammars the worst-case complexity is *cubic* ($O(n^3)$). However, programming languages are usually designed in such a way that their parsing is linear. This means that they use a restricted subset of context-free grammars, but still large enough to deal with matching parentheses and other common programming language features.

We will return to the parsing problem of full context-free grammars later. We first look at the parsing techniques used in compilers, which work for some grammars only. In general, these techniques work for grammars that don't have **ambiguity**. That is, every string has at most one tree. This is not true for context-free grammars in general, but it is guaranteed for most programming languages by design. For parsing, the lack of ambiguity means that the algorithm can stop looking for alternative analyses as soon as it has found one, which is one ingredient of efficiency.

3.6   LL(k) parsing

The simplest practical way to parse programming languages is **LL(k)**, i.e. *left-to-right parsing, leftmost derivations, lookahead k*. It is also called **recursive descent parsing** and has sometimes been used for implementing parsers by hand, that is, without the need of parser generators. The **parser combinators** of Haskell are related to this method. We will take a look at them in Section 8.6.

The idea of recursive descent parsing is the following: for each category, write a function that inspects the first token and tries to construct a tree. Inspecting one token means that the **lookahead** is one; LL(2) parsers inspect two tokens, and so on.

Here is an example grammar:

```
SIf.    Stm ::= "if" "(" Exp ")" Stm ;
SWhile. Stm ::= "while" "(" Exp ")" Stm ;
SExp.   Stm ::= Exp ;
EInt.   Exp ::= Integer ;
```

We need to build two functions, which look as follows in pseudocode. They read the input token by token, and use the variable *next* to point to the next token:

> *Stm pStm()* :
>   **if** (*next* = "if") ... // *try to build tree with SIf*
>   **if** (*next* = "while") ... // *try to build tree with SWhile*
>   **if** (*next is integer*) ... // *try to build tree with SExp*
>
> *Exp pExp()* :
>   **if** (*next is integer k*) **return** *SExp k*

To fill the three dots in this pseudocode, we proceed item by item in each production. If the item is a nonterminal C, we call the parser *pC*. If it is a terminal, we just check that this terminal is the next input token, but don't save it (since we are constructing an *abstract* syntax tree!). For this, the helper function *ignore* is used. Then, for instance, the first branch in the statement parser is the following:

> *Stm pStm()* :
>   **if** (*next* = "if")
>   *ignore*("if")
>   *ignore*("(")
>   *Exp e* := *pExp()*
>   *ignore*(")")
>   *Stm s* := *pStm()*
>   **return** *SIf*(*e, s*)

Thus we save the expression e and the statement s and build an *SIf* three from them, ignoring the terminals in the production.

The pseudocode shown is easy to translate to both imperative and functional code. But we don't recommend this way of implementing parsers, since BNFC is easier to write and more powerful. We show it rather because it is a useful introduction to the concept of **conflicts**, which arise even when BNFC is used.

As an example of a conflict, consider the rules for `if` statements with and without `else`:

```
SIf.     Stm ::= "if" "(" Exp ")" Stm
SIfElse. Stm ::= "if" "(" Exp ")" Stm "else" Stm
```

In an LL(1) parser, which rule should we choose when we see the token `if`? As there are two alternatives, we have a conflict.

One way to solve conflicts is to write the grammar in a different way. In this case, for instance, we can use **left factoring**, which means sharing the common left part of the rules:

```
SIE.    Stm  ::= "if" "(" Exp ")" Stm Rest
RElse.  Rest ::= "else" Stm
REmp.   Rest ::=
```

To get the originally wanted abstract syntax, we have to define a function (in the host language, i.e. Haskell or Java) that eliminates `Rest` trees in the following way:

```
        SIE exp stm REmp          ⟹   SIf exp stm
        SIE exp stm (RElse stm2)  ⟹   SIfElse exp stm stm2
```

But it can be tricky to rewrite a grammar so that it enables LL(1) parsing. Perhaps the most well-known problem is **left recursion**. A rule is left-recursive if it has the form

$$C ::= C \ldots$$

that is, the value category C is itself the first item on the right hand side. Left recursion is common in programming languages, because operators such as `+` are left associative. For instance, consider the simplest pair of rules for sums of integers:

```
Exp ::= Exp "+" Integer
Exp ::= Integer
```

These rules make an LL(1) parser loop, because, to build an `Exp`, the parser first tries to build an `Exp`, and so on. No input is consumed when trying this, and therefore the parser loops.

The grammar can be rewritten, again, by introducing a new category:

```
Exp  ::= Integer Rest
Rest ::= "+" Integer Rest
Rest ::=
```

The new category `Rest` has **right recursion**, which is harmless. A tree conversion is of course needed to return the originally wanted abstract syntax.

The clearest way to see conflicts and to understand the nature of LL(1) parsing is to build a **parser table** from the grammar. This table has a row for each category and a column for each token. Each cell shows what rule applies when the category is being sought and the input begins with the token. For example, the grammar (already considered above)

```
SIf.    Stm ::= "if" "(" Exp ")" Stm ;
SWhile. Stm ::= "while" "(" Exp ")" Stm ;
SExp.   Stm ::= Exp ";" ;
EInt.   Exp ::= Integer ;
```

produces the following table:

-	if	while	integer	(	)	;	$ (END)
Stm	SIf	SWhile	SExp	-	-	-	-
Exp	-	-	EInt	-	-	-	-

A conflict means that a cell contains more than one rule. This grammar has no conflicts, but if we added the `SIfElse` rule, the cell (Stm,if) would contain both `SIf` and `SIfElse`.

Exercise 3-5. Write a recursive-descent parser for the example grammar (with `if`, `while`, expression statements, and integer expressions) in a general-purpose language like Haskell or Java.

3.7 LR(k) parsing

Instead of LL(1), the standard Yacc-like parser tools use **LR(k)**, i.e. *left-to-right parsing, rightmost derivations, lookahead k.* Both algorithms thus read their input left to right. But LL builds the trees from left to right, LR from right to left. The mention of **derivations** refers to the way in which a string can be built by expanding the grammar rules. Thus the **leftmost derivation** of `while(1) if (0) 6 ;` always fills in the leftmost nonterminal first.

```
Stm --> while ( Exp ) Stm
    --> while (   1 ) Stm
    --> while (   1 ) if ( Exp ) Stm
    --> while (   1 ) if (   0 ) Stm
```

```
--> while (   1 ) if (   0 ) Exp ;
--> while (   1 ) if (   0 )   6 ;
```

The **rightmost derivation** of the same string fills in the rightmost nonterminal first.

```
Stm --> while ( Exp ) Stm
    --> while ( Exp ) if ( Exp ) Stm
    --> while ( Exp ) if ( Exp ) Exp ;
    --> while ( Exp ) if ( Exp )   6 ;
    --> while ( Exp ) if (   0 )   6 ;
    --> while (   1 ) if (   0 )   6 ;
```

The LR(1) parser reads its input, and builds a **stack** of results, which are combined afterwards, as soon as some grammar rule can be applied to the top of the stack. When seeing the next token (lookahead 1), it chooses among five **actions**:

- **Shift**: read one more token (i.e. move it from input to stack).

- **Reduce**: pop elements from the stack and replace by a value.

- **Goto**: jump to another state and act accordingly.

- **Accept**: return the single value on the stack when no input is left.

- **Reject**: report that there is input left but no action to take, or that the input is finished but the stack is not one with a single value of expected type.

Shift and reduce are the most common actions, and it is customary to illustrate the parsing process by showing the sequence of these actions. Take, for instance, the following grammar. We use integers as rule labels, so that we also cover the dummy coercion (label 2).

```
1. Exp  ::= Exp "+" Exp1
2. Exp  ::= Exp1
3. Exp1 ::= Exp1 "*" Integer
4. Exp1 ::= Integer
```

The string 1 + 2 * 3 is parsed as follows:

stack	input	action
	1 + 2 * 3	shift
1	+ 2 * 3	reduce 4
Exp1	+ 2 * 3	reduce 2
Exp	+ 2 * 3	shift
Exp +	2 * 3	shift
Exp + 2	* 3	reduce 4
Exp + Exp1	* 3	shift
Exp + Exp1 *	3	shift
Exp + Exp1 * 3	3	reduce 3
Exp + Exp1		reduce 1
Exp		accept

Initially, the stack is empty, so the parser must *shift* and put the token 1 to the stack. The grammar has a matching rule, rule 4, and so a *reduce* is performed. Then another reduce is performed by rule 2. Why? This is because the next token (the lookahead) is +, and there is a rule that matches the sequence Exp +. If the next token were *, then the second reduce would not be performed. This is shown later in the process, when the stack is Exp + Exp1.

How does the parser know when to shift and when to reduce? Like in the case of LL(k) parsing, it uses a table. In an LR(1) table, the rows are **parser states**, and there is a column for each terminal and also for each nonterminal. The cells are parser actions.

So, what is a parser state? It is a grammar rule together with the position that has been reached when trying to match the rule. This position is conventionally marked by a dot. Thus, for instance,

```
Stm ::= "if" "(" . Exp ")" Stm
```

is the state where an if statement is being read, and the parser has read the tokens if and (and is about to look for an Exp.

Here is an example of an LR(1) table. It is based on the table produced by BNFC and Happy from the previous grammar, so it is actually a variant called LALR(1); see below. The Happy compiler has added two rules to the grammar: rule (0) that produces integer literal terminals (L_int) from the nonterminal Integer, and a start rule (here unnumbered), which adds the extra token \$ to mark the end of the input. Then also the other rules have to decide what to do if they reach the end of input. We only show the columns for terminals and the corresponding *shift*, *reduce*, and *accept* actions. For *shift*, the next state is given. For *reduce*, the rule number is given.

		+	*	$	L_int
0	(start)	-	-	-	s3
3	Integer -> L_int .	r0	r0	r0	-
4	Exp1 -> Integer .	r4	r4	r4	-
5	Exp1 -> Exp1 . "*" Integer	-	s8	-	-
6	%start_pExp -> Exp . $	s9	-	a	-
	Exp -> Exp . "+" Exp1				
7	Exp -> Exp1 .	r2	s8	r2	-
	Exp1 -> Exp1 . "*" Integer				
8	Exp1 -> Exp1 "*" . Integer	-	-	-	s3
9	Exp -> Exp "+" . Exp1	-	-	-	s3
10	Exp -> Exp "+" Exp1 .	r1	s8	r1	-
	Exp1 -> Exp1 . "*" Integer				
11	Exp1 -> Exp1 "*" Integer .	r3	r3	r3	-

The size of LR(1) tables can be large, because it is the number of rule positions multiplied by the number of tokens and categories. For LR(2), we need the square of the number, which is too large in practice. Even LR(1) tables are usually not built in their full form. Instead, standard tools like Yacc, Bison, CUP, Happy use **LALR(1), look-ahead LR(1)**. In comparison to full LR(1), LALR(1) reduces the number of states by merging some states that are similar to the left of the dot. States 6, 7, and 10 in the above table are examples of this.

In terms of general expressivity, the following inequations hold:

- LR(0) < LALR(1) < LR(1) < LR(2) ...

- LL(k) < LR(k)

That a *grammar* is in LALR(1), or any other of the classes, means that its parsing table has no conflicts. Therefore none of these classes can contain ambiguous grammars.

Exercise 3-6. Trace the LR parsing of the (nonsense) statement

```
while (2 + 5) 3 * 6 * 7 ;
```

in the language which is the same as the language with + and * used in this section, with while statements and expression statements added.

Exercise 3-7. Consider the language 'X'*, i.e. sequences of symbol X. Write two context-free grammars for it: one left-recursive and one right-recursive. With both grammars, trace the LR parsing of the string XXXX. What can you say about the memory consumption of the two processes?

3.8   Finding and resolving conflicts

In a parsing table (LL, LR, LALR), a **conflict** means that there are several items in a cell. In LR and LALR, two kinds of conflicts may occur:

- **shift-reduce conflict**: between shift and reduce actions.

- **reduce-reduce conflict** between two (or more) reduce actions.

The latter are more harmful, but also easier to eliminate. The clearest case is plain ambiguities. Assume, for instance, that a grammar tries to distinguish between variables and constants:

```
EVar.   Exp ::= Ident ;
ECons.  Exp ::= Ident ;
```

Any `Ident` parsed as an `Exp` can be reduced with both of the rules. The solution to this conflict is to remove one of the rules and leave it to the type checker to distinguish constants from variables.

A more tricky case is implicit ambiguities. The following grammar tries to cover a fragment of C++, where a declaration (in a function definition) can be just a type (`DTyp`), and a type can be just an identifier (`TId`). At the same time, a statement can be a declaration (`SDecl`), but also an expression (`SExp`), and an expression can be an identifier (`EId`).

```
SExp.   Stm  ::= Exp ;
SDecl.  Stm  ::= Decl ;
DTyp.   Decl ::= Typ ;
EId.    Exp  ::= Ident ;
TId.    Typ  ::= Ident ;
```

Now the reduce-reduce conflict can be detected by tracing down a chain of rules:

```
Stm -> Exp -> Ident
Stm -> Decl -> Typ -> Ident
```

In other words, an identifier can be used as a statement in two different ways. The solution to this conflict is to redesign the language: `DTyp` should only be valid in function parameter lists, and not as statements! This is actually the case in C++.

As for shift-reduce conflicts, the classical example is the **dangling else**, created by the two versions of `if` statements:

```
SIf.     Stm ::= "if" "(" Exp ")" Stm
SIfElse. Stm ::= "if" "(" Exp ")" Stm "else" Stm
```

The problem arises when `if` statements are nested. Consider the following input and position (.):

```
if (x > 0) if (y < 8) return y ; . else return x ;
```

There are two possible actions, which lead to two analyses of the statement. The analyses are made explicit by braces.

```
shift:   if (x > 0) { if (y < 8) return y ;  else return x ;}
reduce:  if (x > 0) { if (y < 8) return y ;} else return x ;
```

This conflict is so well established that it has become a "feature" of languages like C and Java. It is solved by a principle followed by standard tools: when a conflict arises, always choose shift rather than reduce. But this means, strictly speaking, that the BNF grammar is no longer faithfully implemented by the parser.

Hence, if your grammar produces shift-reduce conflicts, this will mean that some programs that your grammar recognizes cannot actually be parsed. Usually these conflicts are not so "well-understood" ones as the dangling else, and it can take a considerable effort to find and fix them. The most valuable tool in this work are the **info files** generated by some parser tools. For instance, Happy can be used to produce an info file by the flag `-i`:

```
happy -i ParCPP.y
```

The resulting file `ParConf.info` is a very readable text file. A quick way to check which rules are overshadowed in conflicts is to grep for the ignored *reduce* actions:

```
grep "(reduce" ParConf.info
```

Interestingly, conflicts tend to cluster on a few rules. If you have very many, do

```
grep "(reduce" ParConf.info | sort | uniq
```

The conflicts are (usually) the same in all standard tools, since they use the LALR(1) method. Since the info file contains no Haskell, you can use Happy's info file even if you principally work with another tool.

Another diagnostic tool is the **debugging parser**. In Happy,

```
happy -da ParCPP.y
```

When you compile the BNFC test program with the resulting `ParCPP.hs`, it shows the sequence of actions when the parser is executed. With Bison, you can use **gdb** (GNU Debugger), which traces the execution back to lines in the Bison source file.

3.9   The limits of context-free grammars

Parsing with context-free grammars is decidable, with cubic worst-case complexity. However, exponential algorithms are often used because of their simplicity. For instance, the Prolog programming language has a built-in parser with this property. Haskell's **parser combinators** are a kind of embedded language, working in a way similar to Prolog. The method uses recursive descent, just like LL(k) parsers. But this is combined with **backtracking**, so that the parser need not make deterministic choices. Parser combinators can therefore also cope with ambiguity. We will return to them in Section 8.6.

One problem with Prolog and parser combinators—well known in practice— is their unpredictability. Backtracking may lead to exponential behaviour and very slow parsing. Left recursion may lead to non-termination, and it can be hard to detect if implicit. Using parser generators is therefore a more reliable, even though more restricted, way to implement parsers.

But even the full class of context-free grammars is not the whole story of languages. There are some very simple formal languages that are *not* context-free. One example is the **copy language**. Each sentence of this language is two copies of some word, and the word can be arbitrarily long. The simplest copy language has words consisting of just two symbols, a and b:

$$\{ww | w \in (a|b)^*\}$$

Observe that this is *not* the same as the context-free language

```
S ::= W W
W ::= "a" W | "b" W
W ::=
```

In this grammar, there is no guarantee that the two W's are the same.

The copy language is not just a theoretical construct but has an important application in compilers. A common thing one wants to do is to check that every variable is declared before it is used. Language-theoretically, this can be seen as an instance of the copy language:

```
Program ::= ... Var ... Var ...
```

Consequently, checking that variables are declared before use is a thing that cannot be done in the parser but must be left to a later phase.

Of course, being non-context-free is as such not a fatal property of languages. Even though context-sensitive grammars in general might have exponential parsing complexity, it is easy to see that the copy language can be parsed with a linear algorithm. In Chapter 8, we will introduce two grammar formats that can in fact parse the copy language: parser combinators (Section 8.6) and GF (Section 8.11).

Chapter 4

Type Checking

Type checking tries to find out if a program makes sense. This chapter defines the traditional notion of type checking as exemplified by C and Java. While most questions are straightforward, there are some tricky questions such as variable scopes. And while most things in type checking are trivial for a human to understand, Assignment 2 will soon show that it requires discipline and perseverance to make a machine check types automatically.

This chapter provides all the concepts and tools needed for solving Assignment 2, which is a type checker for a fragment of C++.

4.1 The purposes of type checking

The first impression many programmers have of type checking is that it is annoying. You write a piece of code that makes complete sense to you, but you get a stupid type error. For this reason, untyped languages like Lisp, Python, and JavaScript attract many programmers. They trade type errors for run-time errors, which means they spend a larger proportion of time on debugging than on trying to compile, compared to Java or Haskell programmers. Of course, the latter kind of programmers learn to appreciate type checking, because it is a way in which the compiler can find bugs automatically.

The development of programming languages shows a movement to more and more type checking. This was one of the main novelties of C++ over C. On the limit, a type checker could find *all* errors, that is, all violations of the specification. This is not the case with today's languages, not even the strictest ones like ML and Haskell. In a functional language of today, a sorting function `sort` might have the type

```
sort : List -> List
```

This means that the application `sort([2,1,3])` to a list is type-correct, but the application `sort(0)` to an integer isn't. However, there is nothing that prevents the definition of a sorting function that just returns the same list back. This would be type-correct, even though it wouldn't be a correct sorting function. Surprisingly, even this problem could be solved by a type checker, as is the case in a language such as **Agda**. Agda uses the **propositions as types principle**, which in particular makes it possible to express **specifications as types**. For instance, the sorting function could be declared

```
sort : (x : List) -> (y : List) & Sorted(x,y)
```

where the condition that the value `y` is a sorted version of the argument `x` is expressed as the type `Sorted(x,y)`. But at the time of writing this is still in the avant-garde of programming language technology.

Coming back to more standard languages, type checking has another function completely different from correctness control. It is used for **type annotations**, which means that it enables the compiler to produce more efficient machine code. For instance, JVM has separate instructions for integer and double-precision float addition (`iadd` and `dadd`, respectively). One might always choose `dadd` to be on the safe side, but the code becomes more efficient if `iadd` is used whenever possible. One reason is that integers need just half of the memory doubles need.

Since Java source code uses + ambiguously for integer and float addition, the compiler must decide which one is in question. This is easy if the operands are integer or float constants: it could be made in the parser. But if the operands are variables, and since Java uses the same kind of variables for all types, the parser cannot decide this. Ultimately, recalling Section 3.9, this is so because context-free grammars cannot deal with the copy language! It is the type checker that is aware of the **context**, that is, what variables have been declared and in what types. Luckily, the parser will already have analysed the source code into a tree, so that the task of the type checker is not hopelessly complicated.

4.2   Specifying a type checker

There is no standard tool for type checkers, which means they have to be written in a general-purpose programming language. However, there are standard notations that can be used for specifying the **type system** of a language and easily converted to code in any host language. The most common notation is **inference rules**. An example of an inference rule for C or Java is

$$\frac{a : bool \quad b : bool}{a \,\&\&\, b : bool}$$

which can be read, *if a has type bool and b has type bool. then a* && *b has type bool.*

In general, an inference rule has a set of **premisses** $J_1, \ldots, J_n$ and a **conclusion** J, which are separated by a horizontal line:

$$\frac{J_1 \ \ldots \ J_n}{J}$$

This inference rule is read:

> *From the premisses $J_1, \ldots, J_n$, we can conclude J.*

There is also a shorter paraphrase:

> *If $J_1, \ldots, J_n$, then J.*

In type checkers (and also in interpreters), the rule is often applied upside down:

> *To check J, check $J_1, \ldots, J_n$.*

The premisses and conclusions in inference rules are called **judgements**. The most common judgements in type systems have the form

$$e : T$$

which is read, *expression e has type T.*

4.3   Type checking and type inference

The first step from an inference rule to implementation is pseudo-code for **syntax-directed translation**. Typing rules for expression forms in an abstract syntax are then treated as clauses in a recursive function definition that traverses expression trees. They are read upside down, that is,

> *To check J, check $J_1, \ldots, J_n$.*

which is converted to program code of the format

```
J :
   J₁
   . . .
   Jₙ
```

There are two kinds of functions:

- **Type checking**: given an expression e and a type T, decide if $e : T$.

- **Type inference**: given an expression e, find a type T such that $e : T$.

When we translate a typing rule to type checking code, its conclusion becomes a case for pattern matching, and its premises become recursive calls for type checking. For instance, the above **&&** rule becomes

> $check(a\;\&\&\;b, bool)$:
> > $check(a, bool)$
> > $check(b, bool)$

There are no patterns matching other types than *bool*, so type checking fails for them.

In a type inference rule, the premises become recursive calls as well, but the type in the conclusion becomes the value returned by the function:

> $infer(a\;\&\&\;b)$:
> > $check(a, bool)$
> > $check(b, bool)$
> > **return** *bool*

Notice that the function should not just return bool outright: it must also check that the operands are of type bool.

Both in inference rules and pseudocode, we use concrete syntax notation for expression patterns—that is, $a\&\&b$ rather than $(EAnd\,a\,b)$. In real type checking code, abstract syntax must of course be used.

4.4   Context, environment, and side conditions

How do we type-check variables? Variables symbols like x can have *any* of the types available in a programming language. The type it has in a particular program depends on the **context**. In C and Java, the context is determined by declarations of variables. It is a data structure where one can look up a variable and get its type. So we can think of the context as as **lookup table** of (variable,type) pairs.

In inference rules, the context is denoted by the Greek letter Γ, Gamma. The judgement form for typing is generalized to

$$\Gamma \vdash e : T$$

which is read, *expression e has type T in context* Γ. For example, the following judgement holds:

$$x : \texttt{int}, y : \texttt{int} \vdash x\texttt{+}y\texttt{>}y : \texttt{bool}$$

It means:

> **x + y > y** *is a boolean expression in the context where* **x** *and* **y** *are integer variables.*

Notice the notation for contexts:

$$x_1 : T_1, \ldots, x_n : T_n$$

This notation is handy when writing inference rules, because it allows us to write simply

$$\Gamma, x : T$$

when we add a new variable to the context Γ.

Most typing rules are generalized by adding the same Γ to all judgements, because the context doesn't change.

$$\frac{\Gamma \vdash a : bool \quad \Gamma \vdash b : bool}{\Gamma \vdash a \,\&\&\, b : bool}$$

This would be silly if it was *always* the case. However, as we shall see, the context does change in the rules for type checking declarations.

The places where contexts are needed for expressions are those that involve variables. First of all, the typing rule for variable expressions is

$$\frac{}{\Gamma \vdash x : T} \quad \text{if } x : T \text{ in } \Gamma$$

What does this mean? The condition "if $x : T$ in Γ" is not a judgement but a sentence in the **metalanguage** (English). Therefore it cannot appear above the inference line as one of the premises, but beside the line, as a **side condition**. The situation becomes even cleared if we look at the pseudocode:

> $infer(\Gamma, x)$:
> $t := lookup(x, \Gamma)$
>   **return** t

Looking up the type of the variable is not a recursive call to *infer* or *check*, but uses another function, *lookup*.

One way to make this fully precise is to look at actual implementation code; let's take Haskell code for brevity. Here we have the type inference and lookup functions

```
inferExp  :: Context -> Exp -> Err Type
lookupVar :: Ident  -> Context -> Err Type
```

We also have to make the abstract syntax constructors explicit: we cannot write just x but EVar x, when we infer the type of a variable expression. Then the type inference rule comes out as a pattern matching case in the definition of infer:

```
inferExp gamma (EVar x) = do
  typ <- lookupVar x gamma
  return typ
```

If the language has function definitions, we also need to look up the types of functions when type checking function calls ($f(a, b, c)$). We will assume that the context Γ also includes the type information for functions. Then Γ is more properly called the **environment** for type checking, and not just the context.

The only place where the function storage part of the environment ever changes is when type checking function definitions. The only place where it is needed is when type checking function calls. The typing rule involves a lookup of the function in Γ as a side condition, and the typings of the arguments as premisses:

$$\frac{\Gamma \vdash a_1 : T_1 \quad \cdots \quad \Gamma \vdash a_n : T_n}{\Gamma \vdash f(a_1, \ldots, a_n) : T} \text{ if } f : (T_1, \ldots, T_n) \to T \text{ in } \Gamma$$

For the purpose of expressing the value of function lookup, we use the notation $(T_1, \ldots, T_n) \to T$ for the type of functions, even though there is no such type in the language described.

4.5   Proofs in a type system

Inference rules are designed for the construction of **proofs**, which are structured as **proof trees**. A proof tree can be seen as a trace of the steps that the type checker performs when checking or inferring a type.

Here is a proof tree for the judgement

$$x : \mathtt{int}, y : \mathtt{int} \vdash x\mathtt{+}y\mathtt{>}y : \mathtt{bool}$$

shown in the previous section.

$$\frac{\dfrac{x : \mathtt{int}, y : \mathtt{int} \vdash x : \mathtt{int} \quad x : \mathtt{int}, y : \mathtt{int} \vdash y : \mathtt{int}}{x : \mathtt{int}, y : \mathtt{int} \vdash x\mathtt{+}y : \mathtt{int}} \quad x : \mathtt{int}, y : \mathtt{int} \vdash y : \mathtt{int}}{x : \mathtt{int}, y : \mathtt{int} \vdash x\mathtt{+}y\mathtt{>}y : \mathtt{bool}}$$

The tree can be made more explicit by adding explanations on which rules are applied at each inference:

$$\frac{\dfrac{\overline{x : \mathtt{int}, y : \mathtt{int} \vdash x : \mathtt{int}}^{\;x} \quad \overline{x : \mathtt{int}, y : \mathtt{int} \vdash y : \mathtt{int}}^{\;y}}{x : \mathtt{int}, y : \mathtt{int} \vdash x\mathtt{+}y : \mathtt{int}}^{\;+} \quad \overline{x : \mathtt{int}, y : \mathtt{int} \vdash y : \mathtt{int}}^{\;y}}{x : \mathtt{int}, y : \mathtt{int} \vdash x\mathtt{+}y\mathtt{>}y : \mathtt{bool}}^{\;>}$$

In addition to the variable rule (marked x or y), the tree uses the rules for + and >:

$$\frac{\Gamma \vdash a : int \quad \Gamma \vdash b : int}{\Gamma \vdash a + b : int} \qquad \frac{\Gamma \vdash a : int \quad \Gamma \vdash b : int}{\Gamma \vdash a > b : bool}$$

As we will see in next section, these rules are special cases for rules where also doubles and strings can be added and compared.

4.6 Overloading and type conversions

Variables are examples of expressions that can have different types in different contexts. Another example is **overloaded operators**. The binary arithmetic operations (+ - * /) and comparisons (== != < > <= >=) are in many languages usable for different types.

Let us assume that the possible types for addition and comparisons are int, double, and string. The typing rules then look as follows:

$$\frac{\Gamma \vdash a : t \quad \Gamma \vdash b : t}{\Gamma \vdash a + b : t} \quad \text{if } t \text{ is int or double or string}$$

$$\frac{\Gamma \vdash a : t \quad \Gamma \vdash b : t}{\Gamma \vdash a == b : bool} \quad \text{if } t \text{ is int or double or string}$$

and similarly for the other operators. Notice that a + expression has the same type as its operands, whereas == always gives a boolean. In both cases, we can first infer the type of the first operand and then check the second operand with respect to this type:

$infer(a + b) :$
  $t := infer(a)$
  // *check that* $t \in \{$int, double, string$\}$
  $check(b, t)$
  return t

We have made string a possible type of +, following C++ and Java. For other arithmetic operations, only int and double are possible.

Yet another case of expressions having different type is **type conversions**. For instance, an integer can be converted into a double. This may sound trivial from the ordinary mathematical point of view, because integers are a subset of reals. But for most machines this is not the case, because integers and doubles have totally different binary representations and different sets of instructions. Therefore, the compiler usually has to generate a special instruction for type conversions, both explicit and implicit ones.

The general idea of type conversions involves an ordering between types. An object from a smaller type can be safely (i.e. without loss of information) converted to a larger type, whereas the opposite is not safe. Then, for instance, the typing rule for addition expressions becomes

$$\frac{\Gamma \vdash a : t \;\; \Gamma \vdash b : u}{\Gamma \vdash a+b : max(t,u)} \quad \text{if } t, u \in \{\texttt{int}, \texttt{double}, \texttt{string}\}$$

Let us assume the following ordering:

$$\texttt{int} < \texttt{double} < \texttt{string}$$

Then for instance

$$max(\texttt{int}, \texttt{string}) = \texttt{string}$$

which means that for instance 2 + "hello" must be converted to a string addition, which gives the result 2hello when the expression is evaluated.

Exercise 4-0. The maximum type principle has interesting consequences for the behaviour of expressions. Consider the expression

```
1 + 2 + "hello" + 1 + 2
```

We will return to the details of its evaluation in Chapter 5. But you can already now approach the question by finding out which type of + applies to each of the four additions. Recall that + is left associative!

4.7   The validity of statements and function definitions

Expressions have types, which can be checked and inferred. But what happens when we type-check a statement? Then we are not interested in a type, but just in whether the statement is **valid**. For the validity of a statement, we need a new judgement form,

$$\Gamma \vdash s \;\textit{valid}$$

which is read, *statement s is valid in environment* Γ.

Checking whether a statement is valid often requires type checking some expressions. For instance, in a while statement the condition expression has to be boolean:

$$\frac{\Gamma \vdash e : \textit{bool} \;\; \Gamma \vdash s \;\textit{valid}}{\Gamma \vdash \texttt{while } (e) \;\; s \;\textit{valid}}$$

What about expressions used as statements, for instance, assignments and some function calls? We don't need to care about what the type of the expression is, just that it has one—which means that we are able to infer one. Hence the expression statement rule is

$$\frac{\Gamma \vdash e : t}{\Gamma \vdash e; \;\textit{valid}}$$

A similar rule could be given to **return** statements. However, when they occur within function bodies, they can more properly be checked with respect to the return types of the functions.

Similarly to statements, function definitions are just checked for validity:

$$\frac{x_1 : T_1, \ldots, x_m : T_m \vdash s_1 \ldots s_n \text{ valid}}{T \ f(T_1 \ x_1, \ldots, T_m \ x_m)\{s_1 \ \ldots, s_n\} \text{ valid}}$$

The variables declared as parameters of the function define the context in which the body is checked. The body consists of a list of statements $s_1 \ldots s_n$, which are checked in this context. One can think of this as a shorthand for n premisses, where each statement is in turn checked in the same context. But this is not quite true, because the context may change from one statement to the other. We return to this in next section.

To be really precise, the type checker of function definitions should also check that all variables in the parameter list are distinct. We shall see in the next section that variables introduced in declarations are checked to be new. Then they must also be new with respect to the function parameters.

It would also make sense to add to the conclusion of this rule that Γ is extended by the new function and its type. However, this would not be enough for **mutually recursive functions**, that is, pairs of functions that call each other. Therefore we rather assume that the functions in Γ are added at a separate first pass of the type checker, which collects all functions and their types (and also checks that all functions have different names). We return to this in Section 4.9.

One *could* also add a condition that the function body contains a **return** statement of expected type. A more sophisticated version of this could also allow returns in **if branches**, for example,

```
if (fail()) return 1 ; else return 0 ;
```

4.8   Declarations and block structures

Variables get their types in **declarations**. Each declaration has a **scope**, which is within a certain **block**. Blocks in C and Java correspond roughly to parts of code between curly brackets, { and }. Two principles regulate the use of variables:

1. A variable declared in a block has its scope till the end of that block.

2. A variable can be declared again in an inner block, but not otherwise.

To give an example of these principles at work, let us look at a piece of code with some blocks, declarations, and assignments:

```
{
  int x ;
  {
    x = 3 ;        // x : int
    double x ;     // x : double
    x = 3.14 ;
    int z ;
  }
  x = x + 1 ;      // x : int, receives the value 3 + 1
  z = 8 ;          // ILLEGAL! z is no more in scope
  double x ;       // ILLEGAL! x may not be declared again
  int z ;          // legal, since z is no more in scope
}
```

Our type checker has to control that the block structure is obeyed. This requires a slight revision of the notion of context. Instead of a simple lookup table, Γ must be made into a **stack of lookup tables**. We denote this with a dot notation, for example,

$$\Gamma_1.\Gamma_2$$

where Γ_1 is an old (i.e. outer) context and Γ_2 an inner context. The innermost context is the top of the stack.

The lookup function for variables must be modified accordingly. With just one context, it looks for the variable everywhere. With a stack of contexts, it starts by looking in the top-most context and goes deeper in the stack only if it doesn't find the variable.

A declaration introduces a new variable in the current scope. This variable is checked to be fresh with respect to the context. But how do we express that the new variable is added to the context in which the later statements are checked? This is done by a slight modification of the judgement that a statement is valid: we can write rules checking that a **sequence of statements** is valid,

$$\Gamma \vdash s_1 \ldots s_n \text{ valid}$$

A declaration extends the context used for checking the statements that follow:

$$\frac{\Gamma, x : T \vdash s_2 \ldots s_n \text{ valid}}{\Gamma \vdash T\,x; s_2 \ldots s_n \text{ valid}} \quad x \text{ not in the top-most context in } \Gamma$$

In other words: a declaration followed by some other statements $s_2 \ldots s_n$ is valid, if these other statements are valid in a context where the declared variable is added. This addition causes the type checker to recognize the effect of the declaration.

For block statements, we push a new context on the stack. In the rule notation, this is seen as the appearance of a dot after Γ. Otherwise the logic is similar to the declaration rule—but now, it is the statements inside the block that are affected by the context change, not the statements after:

$$\frac{\Gamma . \vdash r_1 \ldots r_m \text{ valid} \quad \Gamma \vdash s_2 \ldots s_n \text{ valid}}{\Gamma \vdash \{r_1 \ldots r_m\} s_2 \ldots s_n \text{ valid}}$$

Exercise 4-1. Build a proof tree for the judgement

$$\vdash \texttt{int x ; x = x + 1 ;} \ valid$$

This is a proof from the **empty context**, which means no variables are given beforehand. You must first formulate the proper rules of assignment expressions and integer literals, which we haven't shown. But they are easy.

Exercise 4-2. In C++, `for` loops typically have the form

> `for` (*initialization* ; *condition* ; *change*) *statement*

where the *initialization* part declares a new variable, which has its scope inside the `for` loop only. For example,

> `for (int i = 1 ; i < 101 ; i++) printInt(i) ;`

Write a typing rule for this kind of `for` loops. You should require the *condition* to be a boolean expression, but you don't need to assume anything about the *change* expression.

4.9 Implementing a type checker

Implementing a type checker is our first large-scale lesson in **syntax-directed translation**. As shown in Section 4.3, this is done by means of inference and checking functions, together with some auxiliary functions for dealing with contexts in the way shown in Section 4.4. The block structure (Section 4.8) creates the need for some more. Here is a summary of the functions we need:

Type	infer	$(Env\ \Gamma, Exp\ e)$	*infer type of Exp*
Void	check	$(Env\ \Gamma, Exp\ e, Type\ t)$	*check type of Exp*
Void	check	$(Env\ \Gamma, Stms\ s)$	*check sequence of stms*
Void	check	$(Env\ \Gamma, Def\ d)$	*check function definition*
Void	check	$(Program\ p)$	*check a whole program*
Type	lookup	$(Ident\ x, Env\ \Gamma)$	*look up variable*
FunType	lookup	$(Ident\ f, Env\ \Gamma)$	*look up function*
Env	extend	$(Env\ \Gamma, Ident\ x, Type\ t)$	*extend Env with variable*
Env	extend	$(Env\ \Gamma, Def\ d)$	*extend Env with function*
Env	newBlock	$(Env\ \Gamma)$	*enter new block*
Env	emptyEnv	$()$	*empty environment*

We make the *check* functions return a *Void*. Their job is to go through the code and silently return if the code is correct. If they encounter an error, they emit an error message. So does *infer* if type inference fails, and *lookup* if the variable or function is not found in the environment. The *extend* functions can be made to fail if the inserted variable or function name already exists in the environment.

Most of the types involved in the signature above come from the abstract syntax of the implemented language, hence ultimately from its BNF grammar. The exceptions are *FunType*, and *Env*. *FunType* is a data structure that contains a list of argument types and a value type. *Env* contains a lookup table for functions and a stack of contexts, each of which is a lookup table. These are our first examples of **symbol tables**, which are needed in all compiler components after parsing. We don't need the definitions of these types in the pseudocode, but just the functions for lookup and for environment construction (*extend*, *newBlock*, and *emptyEnv*). But we will show possible Haskell and Java definitions below.

Here is the pseudocode for the function checking that a whole program is valid. A program is a sequence of function definitions. It is checked in two passes: first, collect the type signatures of each function by running `extend` on each definition in turn. Secondly, check each function definition in the environment that now contains all the functions with their types.

$$check(d_1, \ldots, d_n) :$$
$$\Gamma_0 := emptyEnv()$$
$$for\ i = 1, \ldots, n : \Gamma_i := extend(\Gamma_{i-1}, d_i)$$
$$for\ each\ i = 1, \ldots, n : check(\Gamma_n, d_i)$$

We first use the `extend` function to update the environment with the types of all functions. Then we check all definitions, on the last line, in the resulting environment Γ_n, because the variables in each definition are not visible to other definitions.

Checking a single function definition is derived from the rule in Section 4.7:

$$check(\Gamma, t\ f\ (t_1\ x_1, \ldots, t_m\ x_m)\{s_1 \ldots s_n\} :$$
$$\Gamma_0 := \Gamma$$
$$for\ i = 1, \ldots, m : \Gamma_i := extend(\Gamma_{i-1}, x_i, t_i)$$
$$check(\Gamma_m, s_1 \ldots s_n)$$

Checking a statement list needs pattern matching over different forms of statements. The most critical parts are declarations and blocks:

$$check(\Gamma, t\ x; s_2 \ldots s_n) :$$
$$// \ here, \ check \ that \ x \ is \ not \ yet \ in \ \Gamma$$
$$\Gamma' := extend(\Gamma, x, t)$$
$$check(\Gamma', s_2 \ldots s_n)$$

$$check(\Gamma, \{r_1 \ldots r_m\}s_2 \ldots s_n) :$$
$$\Gamma' := newBlock(\Gamma)$$
$$check(\Gamma', r_1 \ldots r_m)$$
$$check(\Gamma, s_2 \ldots s_n)$$

Other statements work in a constant environment, just following the rules of Section 4.7.

Exercise 4-3. Using the pseudocode of this section, write the typing rules for `while` statements, expression statements, assignment expressions, and overloaded additions.

4.10 Annotating type checkers

The type checker we have been defining just checks the validity of programs without changing them. But usually the type checker is expected to return a more informative syntax tree to the later phases, a tree with **type annotations**. Then each checking function returns a syntax tree of the same type. For type inference, it is enough to return an expression, because this expression is type annotated, so that the type can be read from it.

Here are the type signatures of an annotating type checker:

Exp	*infer*	$(Env \; \Gamma, Exp \; e)$	*infer type of Exp*
Exp	*check*	$(Env \; \Gamma, Exp \; e, Type \; t)$	*check type of Exp*
Stms	*check*	$(Env \; \Gamma, Stms \; s)$	*check sequence of stms*
Def	*check*	$(Env \; \Gamma, Def \; d)$	*check function definition*
Program	*check*	$(Program \; p)$	*check a whole program*

The abstract syntax needs to be extended with a constructor for type-annotated expressions. We will denote them with $[e : t]$ in the pseudocode. Then, for instance, the type inference rule for addition expression (without type conversions but just overloadings) becomes

$$infer(\Gamma, a + b) :$$
$$[a' : t] := infer(\Gamma, a)$$
$$// \; here, \; check \; that \; t \in \{int, double, string\}$$
$$[b' : t] := check(\Gamma, b, t)$$
$$\textbf{return} \; [a' + b' : t]$$

After running the type checker, syntax trees will have type annotations all over the place, because every recursive call returns an annotated subtree.

An easy way to add type-annotated expressions in the abstract syntax is to use an **internal rule** in BNFC:

```
internal ETyped. Exp ::= "[" Exp ":" Typ "]" ;
```

This rule doesn't add typed expressions to the parser, but only to the abstract syntax, the pretty-printer, and the syntax-directed translation skeleton.

If type conversions are wanted, they can be added by the C++ style rule

```
EConv. Exp ::= Typ "(" Exp ")" ;
```

If this is not made `internal`, also **explicit type conversions** become possible in the language. An implicit conversion adds this to the syntax tree as a part of the type annotation process. For instance, in addition expressions, a conversion is added to the operand that does not have the maximal type:

$$
\begin{aligned}
&infer(\Gamma, a + b) : \\
&\quad [a' : u] := infer(\Gamma, a) \\
&\quad [b' : v] := infer(\Gamma, b) \\
&\quad // \text{ here, check that } u, v \in \{int, double, string\} \\
&\quad \textbf{if } (u < v) \\
&\quad\quad \textbf{return } [v(a') + b' : v] \\
&\quad \textbf{else if } (v < u) \\
&\quad\quad \textbf{return } [a' + u(b') : u] \\
&\quad \textbf{else} \\
&\quad\quad \textbf{return } [a' + b' : u]
\end{aligned}
$$

Exercise 4-4. Give the typing rule and the type-checking pseudocode for explicit type conversions.

4.11   Type checker in Haskell

(Java programmers can safely skip this section and move to Section 4.12.)

The compiler pipeline

To implement the type checker in Haskell, we need three things:

- Define the appropriate auxiliary types and functions.

- Implement type checker and inference functions.

- Put the type checker into the compiler pipeline.

A suitable pipeline looks as follows. It calls the lexer within the parser, and reports a syntax error if the parser fails. Then it proceeds to type checking, showing an error message at failure and saying "OK" if the check succeeds. When more compiler phases are added, the next one takes over from the OK branch of type checking.

```
compile :: String -> IO ()
compile s = case pProgram (myLexer s) of
  Bad err  -> do
    putStrLn "SYNTAX ERROR"
    putStrLn err
    exitFailure
  Ok tree -> case typecheck tree of
    Bad err -> do
      putStrLn "TYPE ERROR"
      putStrLn err
      exitFailure
    Ok _ -> putStrLn "OK"  -- or go to next compiler phase
```

The compiler is implemented in the **IO monad**, which is the most common example of Haskell's monad system. Internally, it will also use an **error monad**, which is here implemented by the **error type** defined in the BNFC generated code (the file ErrM; see Section 2.2):

```
data Err a = Ok a | Bad String
```

The value is either Ok of the expected type or Bad with an error message.

Whatever monad is used, its actions can be **sequenced**. For instance, if

```
checkExp :: Env -> Exp -> Type -> Err ()
```

then you can make several checks one after the other by using do

```
do checkExp env exp1 typ
   checkExp env exp2 typ
```

You can **bind** variables returned from actions, and **return** values.

```
do typ1 <- inferExp env exp1
   checkExp env exp2 typ1
   return typ1
```

If you are only interested in side effects, you can use the dummy value type () (corresponds to void in C and void or Object in Java).

This book is not an introduction to Haskell, so we don't explain the language constructs any more. But it is our common observation that programming language implementation is the place where many Haskell programmers make their first use of monads, if we ignore the basic use of the IO monad. We will use three different monads for the three main tasks: the error monad for the type checker, the IO monad for the interpreter (Chapter 5), and the state monad for the code generator (Chapter 6). One advantage of monads is that their notation comes very close to our imperative pseudocode. Also the BNFC-generated skeleton code (see Section 2.2) is initialized to monadic code.

Symbol tables

The environment has separate parts for the function type table and the stack of variable contexts. We use the Map type for symbol tables, and a list type for the stack. Using lists for symbol tables is also possible, but less efficient and moreover not supported by built-in update functions.

```
type Env = (Sig,[Context])      -- functions and context stack
type Sig = Map Id ([Type],Type) -- function type signature
type Context = Map Id Type       -- variables with their types
```

Auxiliary operations on the environment have the following types:

```
lookupVar :: Env -> Id -> Err Type
lookupFun :: Env -> Id -> Err ([Type],Type)
updateVar :: Env -> Id -> Type -> Err Env
updateFun :: Env -> Id -> ([Type],Type) -> Err Env
newBlock  :: Env -> Env
emptyEnv  :: Env
```

You should keep the datatypes abstract, that is, use them only via these operations. Then you can switch to another implementation if needed, for instance to make it more efficient or add more things in the environment. You can also more easily modify your type checker code to work as an interpreter or a code generator, where the environment is different but the same operations are needed.

Pattern matching for type checking and inference

Here is type inference for some expression forms. Following the skeleton, we use a case expression rather than separate pattern matching equations.

```
inferExp :: Env -> Exp -> Err Type
inferExp env x = case x of
  ETrue    -> return Type_bool
  EInt n   -> return Type_int
  EId id   -> lookupVar env id
  EAdd exp1 exp2 ->
    inferBin [Type_int, Type_double, Type_string] env exp1 exp2
```

Checking the overloaded addition uses a generic auxiliary for overloaded binary operations:

```
inferBin :: [Type] -> Env -> Exp -> Exp -> Err Type
inferBin types env exp1 exp2 = do
```

```
    typ <- inferExp env exp1
    if elem typ types
      then
        checkExp env exp2 typ
      else
        fail $ "wrong type of expression " ++ printTree exp1
```

The BNFC-generated function

```
  printTree :: a -> String
```

converts a syntax tree of any type a to a string using the pretty-printer.

  Checking expressions is defined in terms of type inference:

```
  checkExp :: Env -> Type -> Exp -> Err ()
  checkExp env typ exp = do
    typ2 <- inferExp env exp
    if (typ2 = typ) then
        return ()
      else
        fail $ "type of " ++ printTree exp ++
               "expected " ++ printTree typ ++
               "but found " ++ printTree typ2
```

Here is the statement checker for expression statements, declarations, and
while statements:

```
  checkStm :: Env -> Type -> Stm -> Err Env
  checkStm env val x = case x of
    SExp exp  -> do
      inferExp env exp
      return env
    SDecl typ x  ->
      updateVar env id typ
    SWhile exp stm  -> do
      checkExp env Type_bool exp
      checkStm env val stm
```

Notice that this function is able to change the environment. This means that
the checker for statement lists can be defined simply

```
  checkStms :: Env -> [Stm] -> Err Env
  checkStms env stms = case stms of
    [] -> return env
```

```
x : rest -> do
  env' <- checkStm env x
  checkStms env' rest
```

A seasoned Haskell programmer would of course simply write

```
checkStms = foldM checkStm
```

to get exactly the same function :-)

4.12   Type checker in Java

(Haskell programmers can safely skip this section.)

The visitor pattern

In Section 2.7, we showed a first example of syntax-directed translation in
Java: a calculator defined by adding the eval() method to each abstract syntax class. This is the most straightforward way to implement pattern matching
in Java. However, it is not very modular, because it requires us to go through
and change every class whenever we add a new method. In a compiler, we need
to write a type checker, a code generator, perhaps some optimizations, perhaps an interpreter—and none of these methods would come out as a separate
component.

To solve this problem, Java programmers are recommended to use the **visitor pattern**. It is also supported by BNFC, which generates the **visitor interface** and skeleton code to implement a visitor (see Section 2.2). With this
method, you can put each compiler component into a separate class, which
implements the visitor interface.

This book is not about Java programming, but, in our experience, many
Java programmers see the visitor pattern for the first time when implementing
a programming language—in the same way as Haskell programmers encounter
monads for the first time when they face the same task. Thus we will spend
some time on the visitor concept, which we will moreover meet again in Chapters 5 and 6.

Before attacking the type checker itself, let us look at a simpler example of
the visitor—the calculator. The abstract syntax class Exp generated by BNFC
contains an interface called Visitor, which depends on two class parameters,
A and R. It is these parameters that make the visitor applicable to different
tasks. In type inference, for instance, A is a context and R is a type. Let us
look at the code:

```
public abstract class Exp {
  public abstract <R,A> R accept(Exp.Visitor<R,A> v, A arg);
```

```
  public interface Visitor <R,A> {
    public R visit(Arithm.Absyn.EAdd p, A arg);
    public R visit(Arithm.Absyn.EMul p, A arg);
    public R visit(Arithm.Absyn.EInt p, A arg);
  }
}
public class EAdd extends Exp {
  public final Exp exp_1, exp_2;
  public <R,A> R accept(Arithm.Absyn.Exp.Visitor<R,A> v, A arg) {
    return v.visit(this, arg);
  }
}
public class EInt extends Exp {
  public final Integer integer_;
  public <R,A> R accept(Arithm.Absyn.Exp.Visitor<R,A> v, A arg) {
    return v.visit(this, arg);
  }
}
```

There are three ingredients in the visitor pattern:

- Visitor<R,A>, the interface to be implemented by each application

- R visit(Tree p, A arg), the interface methods in Visitor for each constructor

- R accept(Visitor v, A arg), the abstract class method calling the visitor

Let us see how the calculator is implemented with the visitor pattern:

```
public class Interpreter {
  public Integer eval(Exp e) {
    return e.accept(new Value(), null ) ;
  }
  private class Value implements Exp. Visitor<Integer, Object> {
    public Integer visit (EAdd p, Object arg) {
      return eval(p.exp_1) + eval(p.exp_2) ;
    }
    public Integer visit (EMul p, Object arg) {
      return eval(p.exp_1) * eval(p.exp_2) ;
    }
    public Integer visit (EInt p, Object arg) {
      return p.integer_ ;
    }
  }
}
```

This is the summary of the components involved:

- the return type R is `Integer`.

- the additional argument A is just `Object`; we don't need it for anything.

- the main class is `Interpreter` and contains
  - the public main method, `Integer eval(Exp e)`, calling the visitor with `accept`
  - the private class `Value`, which implements `Visitor` by making the `visit` method evaluate the expression

At least to me, the most difficult thing to understand with visitors is the difference between `accept` and `visit`. It helps to look at what exactly happens when the interpreter is run on an expression—let's say 2 + 3:

```
eval(EAdd(EInt(2),(EInt(3))))              ⟶    eval calls accept
EAdd(EInt(2),(EInt(3))).accept(v,null)     ⟶    accept calls visit
visit(EAdd(EInt(2),(EInt(3))),null)        ⟶    visit calls eval
eval(EInt(2)) + eval(EInt(3))              ⟶    eval calls accept, etc
```

Of course, the logic is less direct than in Haskell's pattern matching:

```
eval (EAdd (EInt 2) (EInt 3))    ⟶    eval calls eval
eval (EInt 2) + eval (EInt 3)    ⟶    eval calls eval, etc
```

But this is how Java can after all make it happen in a modular, type-correct way.

As an optimization, the recursive calls to `eval` in the definition above could be replaced by direct uses of `accept`:

```
public Integer visit (EAdd p, Object arg) {
   return p.exp_1.accept(this,null) + p.exp_2.accept(this,null) ;
}
```

But this would not work for mutually recursive functions such as type inference and type checking.

Type checker components

To implement the type checker in Java, we need three things:

- define the appropriate R and A classes;

- implement type checker and inference visitors with R and A;

- put the type checker into the compiler pipeline.

For the return type R, we already have the class Type from the abstract syntax. But we also need a representation of function types:

```
public static class FunType {
  public LinkedList<Type> args ;
  public Type val ;
}
```

Now we can define the environment with two components: a symbol table (HashMap) of function type signatures, and a stack (LinkedList) of variable contexts. We also need lookup and update methods:

```
public static class Env {
  public HashMap<String,FunType> signature ;
  public LinkedList<HashMap<String,Type>> contexts ;

  public static Type lookupVar(String id) { ...} ;
  public static FunType lookupFun(String id) { ...} ;
  public static void updateVar (String id, Type ty) {...} ;
  // ...
}
```

We also need something that Haskell gives for free: a way to compare types for equality. This we can implement with a special enumeration type of **type codes**:

```
public static enum TypeCode { CInt, CDouble, CString, CBool, CVoid } ;
```

Now we can give the headers of the main classes and methods:

```
public void typecheck(Program p) {
  }
public static class CheckStm implements Stm.Visitor<Env,Env> {
  public Env visit(SDecl p, Env env) {
  }
  public Env visit(SExp p, Env env) {
  }
  // ... checking different statements
public static class InferExp implements Exp.Visitor<Type,Env> {
  public Type visit(EInt p, Env env) {
  }
  public Type visit(EAdd p, Env env) {
  }
  // ... inferring types of different expressions
}
```

On the top level, the compiler ties together the lexer, the parser, and the type
checker. Exceptions are caught at each level:

```
try {
  l = new Yylex(new FileReader(args[0]));
  parser p = new parser(l);
  CPP.Absyn.Program parse_tree = p.pProgram();
  new TypeChecker().typecheck(parse_tree);
} catch (TypeException e) {
    System.out.println("TYPE ERROR");
    System.err.println(e.toString());
    System.exit(1);
} catch (IOException e) {
    System.err.println(e.toString());
    System.exit(1);
} catch (Throwable e) {
    System.out.println("SYNTAX ERROR");
    System.out.println ("At line " + String.valueOf(l.line_num())
  + ", near \"" + l.buff() + "\" :");
    System.out.println("     " + e.getMessage());
    System.exit(1);
}
```

Visitors for type checking

Now, finally, let us look at the visitor code itself. It can be written by modifying
a copy of the BNFC-generated file VisitSkel.java (Section 2.2). Here is
the checker for statements, with declarations and expression statements as
examples:

```
public static class CheckStm implements Stm.Visitor<Env,Env> {
  public Env visit(SDecl p, Env env) {
    env.updateVar(p.id_,p.type_) ;
    return env ;
  }
  public Env visit(SExp s, Env env) {
    inferExp(s.exp_, env) ;
    return env ;
  }
  //...
}
```

Here is an example of type inference, for overloaded multiplication expressions:

```
public static class InferExpType implements Exp.Visitor<Type,Env> {
  public Type visit(demo.Absyn.EMul p, Env env) {
```

```
      Type t1 = p.exp_1.accept(this, env);
      Type t2 = p.exp_2.accept(this, env);
      if (typeCode(t1) == TypeCode.CInt &&
          typeCode(t2) == TypeCode.CInt)
        return TInt;
      else
      if (typeCode(t1) == TypeCode.CDouble &&
          typeCode(t2) == TypeCode.CDouble)
        return TDouble;
      else
        throw new TypeException("Operands to * must be int or double.");
      }
    //...
  }
```

The function `typeCode` converts source language types to their type codes:

```
  public static TypeCode typeCode (Type ty) ...
```

It can be implemented by writing yet another visitor :-)

Chapter 5

Interpreters

This chapter gives the missing pieces of a complete language implementation, enabling you to run your programs and see what they produce. The code for the interpreter turns out to be almost the same as the type checker, thanks to the power of syntax-directed translation. Of course, it is not customary to interpret Java or C directly on source code; but languages like JavaScript are actually implemented in this way, and it is the quickest way to get your language running.

This chapter will also show another kind of an interpreter, one for the Java Virtual Machine (JVM). It is included more for theoretical interest than as a central task in this book. But it will also help you in Chapter 6 to understand the task of generating code for the JVM—in the same way as it helps to know French if you want to write a program that translates English to French.

This chapter provides all the concepts and tools needed for solving Assignment 3, which is an interpreter for a fragment of C++.

5.1 Specifying an interpreter

Just like type checkers, interpreters can be abstractly specified by means of inference rules. The rule system of an interpreter is called the **operational semantics** of the language. The rules tell how to **evaluate** expressions and how to **execute** statements and whole programs.

The basic judgement form for expressions is

$$\gamma \vdash e \Downarrow v$$

which is read, *expression e evaluates to value v in environment γ*. It involves the new notion of **value**, which is what the evaluation returns, for instance, an integer or a double. Values can be seen as a special case of expressions, mostly

consisting of literals; we can also eliminate booleans by defining *true* as the
integer 1 and *false* as 0.

The environment γ (which is a small Γ) now contains values instead of
types. We will denote value environments as follows:

$$x_1 := v_1, \ldots, x_n := v_n$$

When interpreting (i.e. evaluating) a variable expression, we look up its value
from γ. Thus the rule for evaluating variable expressions is

$$\frac{}{\gamma \vdash x \Downarrow v} \quad \text{if } x := v \text{ in } \gamma$$

A possible rule for interpreting multiplication expressions is

$$\frac{\gamma \vdash a \Downarrow u \quad \gamma \vdash b \Downarrow v}{\gamma \vdash a * b \Downarrow u \times v}$$

where $\times$ is multiplication on the level of values. Notice how similar this rule is
to the typing rule of multiplication,

$$\frac{\Gamma \vdash a : t \quad \Gamma \vdash b : t}{\Gamma \vdash a * b : t}$$

One could actually see the typing rule as a special case of interpretation, where
the value of an expression is always its type! From the rule, we can get the
pseudocode for the interpreter,

$$eval(\gamma, a*b) :$$
$$u := eval(\gamma, a)$$
$$v := eval(\gamma, b)$$
$$\textbf{return } u \times v$$

the Haskell code,

```
eval env (EMul a b) = do
  u <- eval env a
  v <- eval env b
  return (u * v)
```

and the Java code,

```
public Integer visit (EMul p, Env env) {
   Integer u = eval(p.exp_1, env) ;
   Integer v = eval(p.exp_2, env) ;
   return u * v ;
}
```

However, we have to add one more thing to these rules and the code so that they
do the job in its full generality. This thing was not needed in type checking:
side effects.

5.2 Side effects

Evaluation can have **side effects**, that is, do things other than just return a value. The most typical side effect is changing the environment. For instance, the assignment expression x = 3 on one hand returns the value 3, on the other changes the value of x to 3 in the environment.

Dealing with side effects needs a more general form of judgement: evaluating an expression returns, not only a value, but also a new environment γ'. We write

$$\gamma \vdash e \Downarrow \langle v, \gamma' \rangle$$

which is read,

> *in environment γ, expression e evaluates to value v and to new environment γ'.*

The original form without γ' could now be seen as a shorthand for the case where $\gamma' = \gamma$.

Now we can write the rule for assignment expressions:

$$\frac{\gamma \vdash e \Downarrow \langle v, \gamma' \rangle}{\gamma \vdash x = e \Downarrow \langle v, \gamma'(x := v) \rangle}$$

The notation $\gamma(x := v)$ means that we **update** the value of x in γ to v, which means that we **overwrite** any old value that x might have had.

Operational semantics is an easy way to explain the difference between **pre-increments** (++x) and **post-increments** (x++). In pre-increment, the value of the expression is $x + 1$. In post-increment, the value of the expression is x. In both cases, x is incremented in the environment. The rules are

$$\frac{}{\gamma \vdash \text{++}x \Downarrow \langle v + 1, \gamma(x := v + 1) \rangle} \quad \text{if } x := v \text{ in } \gamma$$

$$\frac{}{\gamma \vdash x\text{++} \Downarrow \langle v, \gamma(x := v + 1) \rangle} \quad \text{if } x := v \text{ in } \gamma$$

One might think that side effects only matter in expressions that have side effects themselves, such as assignments. But also other forms of expressions must be given all those side effects that occur in their parts. For instance,

$$x\text{++} - \text{++}x$$

is, even if perhaps bad style, an expression that can be interpreted easily with the given rules. The interpretation rule for subtraction just has to take into account the changing environment:

$$\frac{\gamma \vdash a \Downarrow \langle u, \gamma' \rangle \quad \gamma' \vdash b \Downarrow \langle v, \gamma'' \rangle}{\gamma \vdash a - b \Downarrow \langle u - v, \gamma'' \rangle}$$

So, what is the value of x++ - ++x in the environment $x := 1$? This is easy to calculate by building a proof tree:

$$\frac{x := 1 \vdash \text{x++} \Downarrow \langle 1, x := 2 \rangle \quad x := 2 \vdash \text{++x} \Downarrow \langle 3, x := 3 \rangle}{x := 1 \vdash \text{x++ - ++x} \Downarrow \langle -2, x := 3 \rangle}$$

Another kind of side effects are **IO actions**, that is, **input and output**. For instance, printing a value is an output action side effect. We will not treat them with inference rules here, but show later how they can be implemented in the interpreter code.

Exercise 5-0. In C, the evaluation order of the operands of subtraction is left unspecified. What other value could the expression x++ - ++x in the environment $x := 1$ have in C?

5.3 Statements

Statements are executed for their side effects, not to receive values. Lists of statements are executed in order, where each statement may change the environment for the next one. Therefore the judgement form is

$$\gamma \vdash s_1 \dots s_n \Downarrow \gamma'$$

This can, however, be reduced to the interpretation of single statements by the following two rules:

$$\frac{\gamma \vdash s_1 \Downarrow \gamma' \quad \gamma' \vdash s_2 \dots s_n \Downarrow \gamma''}{\gamma \vdash s_1 \dots s_n \Downarrow \gamma''} \qquad \gamma \vdash \; \Downarrow \gamma \quad \text{(empty sequence)}$$

Expression statements just ignore the value of the expression:

$$\frac{\gamma \vdash e \Downarrow \langle v, \gamma' \rangle}{\gamma \vdash e; \Downarrow \gamma'}$$

For if and while statements, the interpreter differs crucially from the type checker, because it has to consider the two possible values of the condition expression. Therefore, if statements have two rules: one where the condition is true (1), one where it is false (0). In both cases, just one of the statements in the body is executed. But recall that the condition can have side effects!

$$\frac{\gamma \vdash e \Downarrow \langle 1, \gamma' \rangle \quad \gamma' \vdash s \Downarrow \gamma''}{\gamma \vdash \text{if } (e) \, s \, \text{else} \, t \Downarrow \gamma''} \qquad \frac{\gamma \vdash e \Downarrow \langle 0, \gamma' \rangle \quad \gamma' \vdash t \Downarrow \gamma''}{\gamma \vdash \text{if } (e) \, s \, \text{else} \, t \Downarrow \gamma''}$$

For while statements, the truth of the condition results in a loop where the body is executed and the condition tested again. Only if the condition becomes false (since the environment has changed) can the loop be terminated.

$$\frac{\gamma \vdash e \Downarrow \langle 1, \gamma' \rangle \quad \gamma' \vdash s \Downarrow \gamma'' \quad \gamma'' \vdash \text{while } (e) \, s \Downarrow \gamma'''}{\gamma \vdash \text{while } (e) \, s \Downarrow \gamma'''} \qquad \frac{\gamma \vdash e \Downarrow \langle 0, \gamma' \rangle}{\gamma \vdash \text{while } (e) \, s \Downarrow \gamma'}$$

Declarations extend the environment with a new variable, which is first given a "null" value. Using this null value in the code results in a run-time error, but this is of course impossible to completely prevent at compile time.

$$\overline{\gamma \vdash t\,x; \Downarrow \gamma, x := null}$$

We don't need to check for the freshness of the new variable, because this has been done in the type checker! This is one instance of the principle of Milner, that "well-typed programs can't go wrong" (Section 1.5). However, in this very case we *would* gain something with a run-time check, if the language allows declarations in branches of if statements.

For block statements, we push a new environment on the stack, just as we did in the type checker. The new variables declared in the block are added to this new environment, which is popped away at exit from the block.

$$\frac{\gamma. \vdash s_1 \ldots s_n \Downarrow \gamma'.\delta}{\gamma \vdash \{s_1 \ldots s_n\} \Downarrow \gamma'}$$

What is happening in this rule? The statements in the block are interpreted in the environment $\gamma.$, which is the same as γ with a new, empty, variable storage on the top of the stack. The new variables declared in the block are collected in this storage, which we denote by δ. After the block, δ is discarded. But the old γ part may still have changed, because the block may have given new values to some old variables! Here is an example of how this works, with the environment after each statement shown in a comment.

```
{
  int x ;        // x := null
  {              // x := null.
    int y ;      // x := null. y := null
    y = 3 ;      // x := null. y := 3
    x = y + y ;  // x := 6. y := 3
  }              // x := 6
  x = x + 1 ;    // x := 7
}
```

5.4 Programs, function definitions, and function calls

How do we interpret whole programs and function definitions? We will assume the C convention that the entire program is executed by running its main function. This means the evaluation of an expression that calls the main function.

Also following C conventions, `main` has no arguments. Thus the execution of a program creates a proof tree whose last line is the judgement

$$\gamma \vdash \texttt{main()} \Downarrow \langle v, \gamma' \rangle$$

The environment γ is the **global environment** of the program. It contains no variables (as we assume there are no global variables). But it does contain all functions. It allows us to look up any function name f and get the parameter list and the function body.

In a function call, we execute the body of the function in an environment where the parameters are given the values of the arguments:

$$\frac{\begin{array}{rl} \gamma & \vdash a_1 \Downarrow \langle v_1, \gamma_1 \rangle \\ \gamma_1 & \vdash a_2 \Downarrow \langle v_2, \gamma_2 \rangle \\ & \cdots \\ \gamma_{m-1} & \vdash a_m \Downarrow \langle v_m, \gamma_m \rangle \\ \gamma.x_1 := v_1, \ldots, x_m := v_m & \vdash s_1 \ldots s_n \Downarrow \langle v, \gamma' \rangle \end{array}}{\gamma \vdash f(a_1, \ldots, a_n) \Downarrow \langle v, \gamma_m \rangle}$$

$$\text{if } t\, f(t_1\, x_1, \ldots, t_m\, x_m)\{s_1\ \ldots, s_n\} \text{ in } \gamma$$

This is quite a mouthful. Let us explain it in detail:

- The first m premisses evaluate the arguments of the function call. As the environment can change, we show m versions of γ.

- The last premiss evaluates the body of the function. This is done in a new environment, which binds the parameters of f to its actual arguments.

- No other variables can be accessed when evaluating the body. Hence the local variables in the body won't be confused with the old variables in γ. Actually, the old variables cannot be updated either. All this is already guaranteed by type checking. Thus the old environment γ is needed here only to look up functions, and using γ_m instead of γ here wouldn't make any difference.

- The value that is returned by evaluating the body comes from the `return` statement in the body.

We have not yet defined how function bodies, which are lists of statements, can return values. We do this by a simple rule saying that the value returned comes from the expression of the last statement, which must be a `return` statement:

$$\frac{\gamma \vdash s_1 \ldots s_{n-1} \Downarrow \gamma' \quad \gamma' \vdash e \Downarrow \langle v, \gamma'' \rangle}{\gamma \vdash s_1 \ldots s_{n-1} \texttt{ return } e \Downarrow \langle v, \gamma'' \rangle}$$

If we want to guarantee that "well-typed programs can't go wrong", we must thus make sure in the type checker that function bodies have returns.

5.5 Laziness

The rule for interpreting function calls is an example of the **call by value** evaluation strategy. This means that the arguments are evaluated *before* the function body is evaluated. Its alternative is **call by name**, which means that the arguments are inserted into the function body as *expressions*, before evaluation. One advantage of call by name is that it doesn't need to evaluate expressions that don't actually occur in the function body. Therefore it is also known as **lazy evaluation**. A disadvantage is that, if the variable is used more than once, it has to be evaluated again and again. This, in turn, is avoided by a more refined technique of **call by need**, which is the one used in Haskell.

We will return to evaluation strategies in Section 7.5. Most languages, in particular C and Java, use call by value, which is why we have used it here, too. But even these languages do have some exceptions: the boolean expressions a && b and a || b are evaluated lazily. Thus in a && b, a is evaluated first. If the value is false (0), the whole expression comes out false, and b is not evaluated at all. This is actually important, because it allows the programmer to write

```
x != 0 && 2/x > 1
```

which would otherwise result in a division-by-zero error when x == 0.

The operational semantics resembles `if` and `while` statements in Section 5.3. Thus it is handled with two rules—one for the 0 case and one for the 1 case:

$$\frac{\gamma \vdash a \Downarrow \langle 0, \gamma' \rangle}{\gamma \vdash a\&\&b \Downarrow \langle 0, \gamma' \rangle} \qquad \frac{\gamma \vdash a \Downarrow \langle 1, \gamma' \rangle \quad \gamma' \vdash b \Downarrow \langle v, \gamma'' \rangle}{\gamma \vdash a\&\&b \Downarrow \langle v, \gamma'' \rangle}$$

For a || b, the evaluation stops if a == 1.

5.6 Implementing the interpreter

The code for the interpreter is mostly a straightforward variant of the type checker. The biggest difference is in the return types, and in the contents of the environment:

$\langle Val, Env \rangle$	*eval*	$(Env\ \gamma, Exp\ e)$
Env	*exec*	$(Env\ \gamma, Stm\ s)$
Void	*exec*	$(Program\ p)$
Val	*lookup*	$(Ident\ x, Env\ \gamma)$
Def	*lookup*	$(Ident\ f, Env\ \gamma)$
Env	*extend*	$(Env\ \gamma, Ident\ x, Val\ v)$
Env	*extend*	$(Env\ \gamma, Def\ d)$
Env	*newBlock*	$(Env\ \gamma)$
Env	*exitBlock*	$(Env\ \gamma)$
Env	*emptyEnv*	$()$

The top-level interpreter first gathers the function definitions to the environment, then executes the `main` function:

$$exec(d_1 \ldots d_n):$$
$$\quad \gamma_0 := emptyEnv()$$
$$\quad \textbf{for } i = 1, \ldots, n:$$
$$\quad\quad \gamma_i := extend(\gamma_{i-1}, d_i)$$
$$\quad eval(\gamma_n, \texttt{main}())$$

Executing statements and evaluating expressions follows from semantic rules in the same way as type checking follows from typing rules. In fact, it is easier now, because we don't have to decide between type checking and type inference. Here are some examples:

$$exec(\gamma, e;):$$
$$\quad \langle v, \gamma' \rangle := eval(\gamma, e)$$
$$\quad \textbf{return } \gamma'$$

$$exec(\gamma, \texttt{while } (e)\ s):$$
$$\quad \langle v, \gamma' \rangle := eval(\gamma, e)$$
$$\quad \textbf{if } v = 0$$
$$\quad\quad \textbf{return } \gamma'$$
$$\quad \textbf{else}$$
$$\quad\quad \gamma'' := exec(\gamma', s)$$
$$\quad\quad exec(\gamma'', \texttt{while } (e)\ s)$$

$$eval(\gamma, a - b):$$
$$\quad \langle u, \gamma' \rangle := eval(\gamma, a)$$
$$\quad \langle v, \gamma'' \rangle := eval(\gamma', b)$$
$$\quad \textbf{return } \langle u - v, \gamma'' \rangle$$

$$eval(\gamma, f(a_1, \ldots, a_m)):$$
$$\quad \textbf{for } i = 1, \ldots, m:$$
$$\quad\quad \langle v_i, \gamma_i \rangle := eval(\gamma_{i-1}, a_i)$$
$$\quad t\ f(t_1\ x_1, \ldots, t_m\ x_m)\{s_1 \ldots s_n\} := lookup(f, \gamma)$$
$$\quad \langle v, \gamma' \rangle := eval(x_1 := v_1, \ldots, x_m := v_m, s_1 \ldots s_n)$$
$$\quad \textbf{return} \langle v, \gamma_m \rangle$$

The implementation language takes care of the operations on values, for instance, comparisons like $v = 0$ and calculations like $u - v$.

The implementation language may also need to define some **predefined functions**, in particular ones used for input and output. Six such functions are needed in Assignment 3 of this book: reading and printing integers, doubles, and strings. The simplest way to implement them is as special cases of the `eval` function, calling the host language printing or reading functions:

$$eval(\gamma, \texttt{printInt}(e)):$$
$$\langle\gamma', v\rangle := eval(\gamma, e)$$
// print integer v to standard output
return $\langle void\text{-}value, \gamma'\rangle$

$$eval(\gamma, \texttt{readInt}()):$$
// read integer v from standard input
return $\langle v, \gamma\rangle$

The type `Val` can be thought of as a special case of `Exp`, only containing literals (and negative numbers), but it is better implemented as an algebraic data type. One way to do this is to derive the implementation from a BNFC grammar by `internal` rules (cf. Section 4.10):

```
internal VInteger.   Val ::= Integer ;
internal VDouble.    Val ::= Double ;
internal VString.    Val ::= String ;
internal VVoid.      Val ::= ;
internal VUndefined. Val ::= ;
```

But some work remains to be done with the arithmetic operations. You cannot simply write

```
VInteger(2) + VInteger(3)
```

because + in Haskell and Java is not defined for the type `Val`. Instead, you have to define a special function `addVal` to the effect that

```
addVal(VInteger(u),VInteger(v)) = VInteger(u+v)
addVal(VDouble(u), VDouble(v))  = VDouble(u+v)
addVal(VString(u), VString(v))  = VString(u+v)
```

In Java, + will do for strings, but in Haskell you need ++. You won't need any other cases because, once again, *well-typed programs can't go wrong!*

The actual Haskell and Java code follows the same structure as in Chapter 4. In Haskell, the monad needs to be changed: the IO monad is now the most natural choice. Thus, for instance,

```
execStm :: Env -> Stm -> IO Env
evalExp :: Env -> Exp -> IO (Val,Env)
```

In Java, the corresponding types are

```
class StmExecuter implements Stm.Visitor<Object,Env> {
  public Object visit(CPP.Absyn.SDecl p, Env env)
  ...
class ExpEvaluator implements Stm.Visitor<Val,Env> {
  public Val visit(CPP.Absyn.EAdd p, Env env)
  ...
```

Notice that the Visitor interface requires a return type, which is expectedly set to Val in ExpEvaluator, and to the dummy type Object in StmExecuter. The environment can be changed as a side effect.

Both interpreters can be easily extended to **debuggers**, which print the state (i.e. the values of variables) after each change of the state. They should also print the statement or expression causing the change of the state.

5.7   Interpreting Java bytecode*

It is a common saying that "Java is an interpreted language". We saw already in Chapter 1 that this is not quite true. The truth is that Java is compiled to another language, **JVM**, **Java Virtual Machine** or **Java bytecode**, and JVM is then interpreted.

JVM is very different from Java, and its implementation is quite a bit simpler. In Chapter 1, we saw an example, the execution of the bytecode compiled from the expression 5 + (6 * 7):

```
bipush 5   ; 5
bipush 6   ; 5 6
bipush 7   ; 5 6 7
imul       ; 5 42
iadd       ; 47
```

After ; (the comment delimiter in JVM assembler), we see the **stack** as it evolves during execution. At the end, the value of the expression, 47, is found on the **top** of the stack. In our representation, the "top" is the right-most element.

Like most machine languages, JVM has neither expressions nor statements but just **instructions**. Here is a selections of instructions that we will use in the next chapter to compile into:

instruction	explanation
bipush n	push byte constant n
iadd	pop topmost two values and push their sum
imul	pop topmost two values and push their product
iload i	push value stored in address i
istore i	pop topmost value and store it in address i
goto L	go to code position L
ifeq L	pop top value; if it is 0 go to position L

The instructions working on integers have variants for other types in the full JVM; see next chapter, and also Appendix B for a longer list.

The load and store instructions are used to compile variables. The code generator assigns a **memory address** to every variable. This address is an integer. Declarations are compiled so that the next available address is reserved to the variable in question; no instruction is generated. Using a variable as an expression means loading it, whereas assigning to it means storing it. The following code example with both C and JVM illustrates the workings:

```
int i ;            ; reserve address 0 for i, no code generated
i = 9 ;            bipush 9
                   istore 0
int j = i + 3 ;    ; reserve address 1 for j
                   iload 0
                   bipush 3
                   iadd
                   istore 1
```

Control structures such as while loops are compiled to **jump instructions**: goto, which is an **unconditional jump**, and ifeq, which is a **conditional jump**. The jumps go to **labels**, which are positions in the code. Here is how while statements can be compiled:

```
                   TEST:
while (exp)          ; here, code to evaluate exp
  stm                ifeq END
                     ; here, code to execute stm
                     goto TEST
                   END:
```

We have been explaining the JVM in informal English. To build an interpreter, it is useful to have formal semantics. This time, the semantics is built by the use of **transitions**: simple rules that specify what each instruction does. This kind of semantics is also known as **small-step semantics**, as each rule specifies just one step of computation. The operational semantics for C/Java source code that we gave earlier in this chapter is correspondingly called **big-step semantics**. For instance, a + b is there specified by saying a and b are evaluated first; but each of them can take any number of intermediate steps.

The format of our small-step rules for JVM is

$$\langle Instruction, Env \rangle \longrightarrow \langle Env' \rangle$$

The environment Env has the following parts:

- a **code pointer** P,

- a **stack** S,

- a **variable storage** V.

The rules work on instructions, executed one at a time. The next instruction is determined by the code pointer. Each instruction can do some of the following:

- increment the code pointer: $P + 1$

- change the code pointer according to a label: $P(L)$

- copy a value from a storage address: $V(i)$

- write a value in a storage address: $V(i := v)$

- push values on the stack: $S.v$

- pop values from the stack

Here are the small-step semantic rules for the instructions we have introduced:

$$
\begin{array}{lllll}
\langle \text{bipush } v, & P, V, S \rangle & \longrightarrow & \langle P+1, & V, & S.v \rangle \\
\langle \text{iadd}, & P, V, S.v.w \rangle & \longrightarrow & \langle P+1, & V, & S.v + w \rangle \\
\langle \text{imul}, & P, V, S.v.w \rangle & \longrightarrow & \langle P+1, & V, & S.v \times w \rangle \\
\langle \text{iload } i, & P, V, S \rangle & \longrightarrow & \langle P+1, & V, & S.V(i) \rangle \\
\langle \text{istore } i, & P, V, S.v \rangle & \longrightarrow & \langle P+1, & V(i := v), & S \rangle \\
\langle \text{goto } L, & P, V, S \rangle & \longrightarrow & \langle P(L), & V, & S \rangle \\
\langle \text{ifeq } L, & P, V, S.0 \rangle & \longrightarrow & \langle P(L), & V, & S \rangle \\
\langle \text{ifeq } L, & P, V, S.v \rangle & \longrightarrow & \langle P(L), & V, & S \rangle \ (v \neq 0) \\
\end{array}
$$

In fact, the big-step relation $\Downarrow$ can be seen as the **transitive closure** of the small-step relation $\longrightarrow$:

$e \Downarrow v$ means that $e \longrightarrow \ldots \longrightarrow v$ in some number of steps.

In the JVM case $e \Downarrow v$ means that executing the instructions in e returns the value v on top of the stack after some number of steps and then terminates. To make this completely precise, we should of course also specify how the environment evolves.

Semantic rules are a precise, declarative specification of an interpreter. They can guide its implementation. But they also make it possible, at least in principle, to perform **reasoning about compilers**. If both the source language and the target language have a formal semantics, it is possible to define the **correctness of a compiler** precisely. For instance:

> An expression compiler c is *correct* if, for all expressions e, $e \Downarrow v$ if and only if $c(e) \Downarrow v$.

Of course, it is a substantial task actually to carry out such a verification. To start with, one has to make sure that arithmetic operations work in the same way in the source and the target language. The machine's representation of integers is finite (for instance, 32 bits), which requires a careful specification of what happens with an overflow. Floating-point arithmetic is even more complex. In this book, we have not worried about such details. It might happen that, for instance, interpreters written in Haskell and Java produce different values in certain limiting cases.

Exercise 5-1.+ Implement an interpreter for a fragment of JVM, permitting the execution of at least straight-code programs (i.e. programs without jumps). You can work on text files with assembly code.

5.8   Objects and memory management*

The previous section explained a part of JVM in which integers are the only possible values. If doubles are added, we get a set of new instructions, which for the most part just duplicate the integer instructions: **dadd** for addition, **dload** for loading a variable; Section 6.4 and Appendix B give more details. The interpretation of these instructions is similar to the integer instructions, with an important modification: the **size** of **double** values is twice the size of **int** values. Thus when a **double** is pushed on the stack, or stored in the memory, it occupies two "slots" (32-bit memory words) instead of one. There's also a danger of, for instance, by mistake treating a **double** as two integers and doing things like popping a half of a **double** from the stack. This never happens if the JVM code is generated by a type-checking compiler, but could happen in code created in some other way, and should then be captured by **bytecode verification**. Bytecode verification can be seen as a light-weight type checking carried out by JVM before it executes a class file.

The size of values depends on type, and it is not restricted to one or two memory words. In fact, there are types with *no* fixed size. The type **string**

is an example: if you declare a string variable, the size of its value can grow
beyond any limits when the program is running. This is usually the case with
objects, which Java manipulates by using complex types, **classes**.

The compilation of object-oriented programs in full generality is beyond the
scope of this book. But we can get a flavour of the issues by just looking at
strings. Consider the function that replicates a string k times:

```
string replicate(int k, string s) {
  string r ;
  r = s ;
  int i = 1 ;
  while (i < k){
    r = s + r ;
    i++ ;
  }
  return r ;
}
```

What happens when the string variable **r** is declared is that one memory word
is allocated to store an **address**. Loading **r** on the stack means loading just
this address—which has the same size as an integer, independently of the size
of the string itself. The address indicates the place where the string itself is
stored. It is not stored on the stack, but in another part of the memory, called
the **heap**. Let us look at what happens when the program is running with k
$= 2$, $s = "hi"$. We have to consider the "ordinary" variable storage (V, as in
the semantic rules above) and the heap separately. The evolution of the stack
and the heap is shown in Figure 5.1.

The variables that have their values in V, such as integer variables, are
called **stack variables**. In the current example, k and i are stack variables,
occupying addresses 0 and 3, respectively. Stack variables store objects of fixed
sizes, neatly piled on top of each other. But s and r are **heap variables**. For
them, V stores just addresses to the heap. In the heap, the addresses point to
objects of variable sizes. They can be shared (as in the case where s and r point
to the same string) or have some shared parts, with links to other segments
of data. They must in general be split around in different places in the heap,
because any amount of storage reserved for them may get insufficient. We will
not go into the details of how exactly strings are stored; the essential thing is
that an object on the heap need not be stored "in one place".

The stack and the stack variable storage are allocated separately for each
function call. When the function terminates (usually by **return**), this storage
is freed. But this does not automatically free the heap storage. For instance, at
the exit from the function **replicate**, the storage for k, s, r, and i is emptied,
and therefore the addresses &s and &r disappear from V. However, we cannot

source	JVM	stack	V	heap
	; k in 0, s in 1	—	2,&s	&s> "hi"
string r ;	; reserve 2 for r	—	2,&s,_	
r = s ;	aload 1	&s		
	astore 2	—	2,&s,&s	
int i = 1 ;	; reserve 3 for i	—	2,&s,&s,_	
	bipush 1	1		
	istore 3	—	2,&s,&s,1	
r = s + r ;	aload 1	&s		
	aload 2	&s.&s		
	; call string-+	&r		&s> "hi",&r> "hihi"
	astore 2		2,&s,&r,1	&s> "hi",&r> "hihi"

Figure 5.1: Stack and heap in string replication.

just take away the strings "hi" and "hihi" from the heap, because they or
their parts may still be accessed by some other stack variables from outer calls.
This means that, while a program is running, its heap storage can grow beyond
all limits, even beyond the physical limits of the computer. To prevent this,
memory management is needed.

In C and C++, memory management is performed manually: the source
code uses the function malloc to reserve a part of memory and obtain a pointer
to the beginning of this part, and the function free to make the memory usable
for later calls of malloc, when it is no longer needed. In C++, the Standard
Template Library tries to hide much of this from the application programmer.

In Java, memory management is automatic, because JVM takes care of it.
The component of JVM that does this is called **garbage collection**. Garbage
collection is a procedure that finds out what parts of the heap are still needed,
in the sense that there are stack variables pointing to them. The parts that
are not needed can be freed for new uses.

Which one is better, manual memory management or garbage collection?
There are many programmers who prefer C-style manual management, because
it can be more precise and thereby consume just the minimum of memory
required, and also because garbage collection is a program that has to be run
beside the main program and can slow it down in unpredictable ways. On
the other hand, garbage collection techniques have improved a lot due to the
development of languages like Java and Haskell, which rely on it. It is so good
that its performance can be hard to beat by manual memory management.

Of course, manual memory management is needed on the implementation
level for languages that need heap allocation and garbage collection. It is

needed for writing the interpreter, as in the case of JVM. In the case of Haskell, which is compiled to native code, garbage collection is a part of the **run-time system**, which is support code linked together with the code of the compiled program itself.

One of the simplest garbage collection methods is the **mark-sweep garbage collection** algorithm. It is based on a **memory model**, which defines the stack and heap data structures. For simplicity, let us think of them both as arrays. In the stack, the array elements are of two kinds:

- data (an integer value)

- heap address (can also be an integer, but distinguishable from data)

The heap is segmented to **blocks**. Each element in the heap is one of:

- beginning of a block, indicating its length (integer) and freeness (boolean)

- data (an integer value)

- heap address (pointing to elsewhere in the heap)

- unused

For instance, an unaddressed block containing an array of the three integers 6, 7, 8 is a heap segment of four elements:

```
begin 3 false, data 6, data 7, data 8
```

After each block, either a new begin node or an unused node must follow.
The algorithm itself composes three functions:

- *roots*: find all heap addresses on the stack

- *mark*: recursively mark as **true** all heap blocks that are addressed

- *sweep*: replace unmarked memory blocks with "unused" cells and unmark marked blocks

The boolean freeness value of beginning elements thus indicates marking in the mark-sweep garbage collection. The mark of the beginning node applies to the whole block, so that the sweep phase either preserves or frees all nodes of the block.

Exercise 5-2.+ Implement the mark-sweep garbage collection algorithm, including a memory model needed for it. More details can be found in e.g. the books *Modern Compiler Implementation* by Appel and *Implementing Functional Languages* by Peyton Jones and Lester, both listed in Appendix D.

Chapter 6

Code Generation

There is a **semantic gap** between the basic constructs of high-level and machine languages. This may make machine languages look frighteningly different from source languages. However, the syntax-directed translation method can be put into use once again, Assignment 4 will be painless for anyone who has completed the previous assignments. It uses JVM, Java Virtual Machine, as target code. For the really brave, we will also give an outline of compilation to native Intel x86 code. This is the last piece in understanding the whole chain from source code to bare silicon. We cannot give the full details, but focus on two features that don't show in the JVM but are important in real machines: how to use registers and how to implement function calls by using stack frames.

This chapter provides all the concepts and tools needed for solving Assignment 4, which is a compiler from a fragment of C++ to JVM.

6.1 The semantic gap

Java and JVM are based on different kinds of constructions. These differences create the **semantic gap**, which a compiler has to bridge. Here is a summary, which works for many other source and target languages as well:

high-level code	machine code
statement	instruction
expression	instruction
variable	memory address
value	bit vector
type	memory layout
control structure	jump
function	subroutine
tree structure	linear structure

The general picture is that machine code is simpler. This is what makes the correspondence of concepts into *many-one*: for instance, both statements and expressions are compiled to instructions. The same property makes compilation of constructs into *one-many*: typically, one statement or expression translates to many instructions. For example,

```
x + 3          iload 0
               bipush 3
               iadd
```

But the good news resulting from this is that compilation is easy, because it can proceed by just *ignoring* some information in the source language!

However, this is not completely true. Machine languages also need some information that is not explicit in most source languages, but must be extracted from the code in earlier compilation phases. In particular, the type checker has to annotate the syntax tree with type information as shown in Section 4.10.

6.2 Specifying the code generator

Just like type checkers and interpreters, we could specify a code generator by means of inference rules. The judgement form could be

$$\gamma \vdash e \downarrow c$$

which is read, *expression e generates code c in environment* γ. The rules for compiling $*$ expressions could be

$$\frac{\gamma \vdash a \downarrow c \quad \gamma \vdash b \downarrow d}{\gamma \vdash [a * b : \texttt{int}] \downarrow c\,d\,\texttt{imul}} \qquad \frac{\gamma \vdash a \downarrow c \quad \gamma \vdash b \downarrow d}{\gamma \vdash [a * b : \texttt{double}] \downarrow c\,d\,\texttt{dmul}}$$

thus one rule for each type, and with type annotations assumed to be in place.

However, we will here use only pseudocode rather than inference rules. One reason is that inference rules are not traditionally used for this task, so the notation would be a bit home-made. Another, more important reason is that the generated code is sometimes quite long, and the rules could become too wide to fit on the page. But as always, rules and pseudocode are just two concrete syntaxes for the same abstract ideas.

Following the above rules, the pseudocode for compiling $*$ expressions becomes

$$compile(\gamma, [a * b : t]) :$$
$$c := compile(\gamma, a)$$
$$d := compile(\gamma, b)$$
$$\textbf{if}\, t = int$$

> **return** $c\,d$ imul
> **else**
> **return** $c\,d$ dmul

The type of this function is

> *Code compile(Env γ, Exp e)*

Even this is not the most common and handy way to specify the compiler. We will rather use the following format:

> *Void compile(Exp e)*
> *compile([a * b : t]) :*
>   *compile(a)*
>   *compile(b)*
>   **if** $t = int$
>   *emit(imul)*
>   **else**
>   *emit(dmul)*

This format involves two simplifications:

- the environment is kept implicit—as a global variable, which may be consulted and changed by the compiler;

- code is generated as a side effect—by the function *Void emit(Code c)*, which writes the code into a file.

6.3 The compilation environment

As in type checkers and interpreters, the environment stores information on functions and variables. As suggested in Section 5.7, we also need to generate fresh labels for jump instructions. Thus the environment contains

- for each function, its type in the JVM notation;

- for each variable, its address as an integer;

- a counter for variable addresses;

- a counter for jump labels.

The exact definition of the environment need not bother us in the pseudocode. We just need to know the utility functions that form its interface. Here are the pseudocode signatures for the compilation and helper functions:

Void	compile	(Exp e)
Void	compile	(Stm s)
Void	compile	(Def d)
Void	emit	(Code c)
Address	lookup	(Ident x)
FunType	lookup	(Ident f)
Void	extend	(Ident x, Type t)
Void	extend	(Def d)
Void	newBlock	()
Void	exitBlock	()
Void	emptyEnv	()
Label	newLabel	()

The *newLabel* function gives a fresh label to be used in jump instructions. All labels in the code for a function must be distinct, because they must uniquely identify a code position.

When extending the environment with a new variable, the **size** of its value must be known. For integers, booleans, and strings, the size is 1. For doubles, it is 2. The addresses start from 0, which is given to the first variable declared. The first variables are the function parameters, after which the locals follow. Blocks can overshadow old variables as usual. Here is an example of how the variable storage develops in the course of a function. M is the counter giving the next available address

```
int foo (double x, int y)
{                 // x -> 0, y -> 2                            M=3
   string i ;     // x -> 0, y -> 2, i -> 3,                   M=4
   bool b ;       // x -> 0, y -> 2, i -> 3, b -> 4            M=5
   {              // x -> 0, y -> 2, i -> 3, b -> 4 .          M=5
     double i ;   // x -> 0, y -> 2, i -> 3, b -> 4 . i -> 5   M=7
   }              // x -> 0, y -> 2, i -> 3, b -> 4            M=5
   int z ;        // x -> 0, y -> 2, i -> 3, b -> 4, z -> 5    M=6
}
```

Notice that the maximum value of M is the maximum amount of variable storage needed by the program, here 7. This information is needed when code is generated for each function definition in JVM.

6.4   Simple expressions and statements

The simplest expressions are the integer and double literals. The simplest instructions to compile them to are

- `ldc` *i*, for pushing an integer or a string *i*

- `ldc2_w` d, for pushing a double d

These instructions are implemented in a special way by using a separate storage called the **runtime constant pool**. Therefore they are not the most efficient instructions to use for small numbers: for them, the JVM also has

- `bipush` b, for integers whose size is one byte

- `iconst_m1` for -1, `iconst_0` for 0, ..., `iconst_5` for 5

- `dconst_0` for 0.0, `dconst_1` for 1.0

The `dconst` and `iconst` sets are better than `bipush` because they need no second byte for the argument. It is of course easy to optimize the code generation to one of these. But let us assume, for simplicity, the use of the worst-case instructions:

$compile(i)$: // integer literals
    $emit(\texttt{ldc } i)$

$compile(d)$: // double literals
    $emit(\texttt{ldc2\_w } d)$

$compile(s)$: // string literals
    $emit(\texttt{ldc } s)$

Arithmetic operations were already covered. The scheme shown for multiplication in Section 6.2 works also for subtraction and division. For addition, we need one more case: string concatenation is compiled as a function call (`invokestatic`, cf. Section 6.7):

$compile([a + b : t])$:
    $compile(a)$
    $compile(b)$
    if $t = int$
      $emit(\texttt{iadd})$
    elseif $t = double$
      $emit(\texttt{dadd})$
    else
      $emit(\texttt{invokestatic runtime/plusString(Ljava/lang/String;}$
                        $\texttt{Ljava/lang/String;)Ljava/lang/String;)}$

Variables are loaded from the storage:

$compile([x : int])$: $emit(\texttt{iload } lookup(x))$
$compile([x : double])$: $emit(\texttt{dload } lookup(x))$
$compile([x : string])$: $emit(\texttt{aload } lookup(x))$

Like for constants, there are special instructions available for small addresses; see Appendix B.

Assignments need some care, since we are treating them as expressions which both have side effects and return values. A simple-minded compilation would give

```
i = 3 ; ⟹ iconst_3 istore_1
```

It follows from the semantics in Section 5.7 that after `istore`, the value 3 is no more on the stack. This is fine as long as the expression is used only as a statement. But if its value is needed, then we need both to store it and have it on the stack. One way to guarantee this is

```
iconst_3 istore_1 iload_1
```

Another way is to **duplicate** the top of the stack with the instruction dup:

$$\langle \mathrm{dup}, P, V, S.v \rangle \longrightarrow \langle P+1, V, S.v.v \rangle$$

This works for integers and strings; the variant for doubles is dup2. Thus we can use the following compilation scheme for assignments:

$compile([x = e : t])$:
   $compile(e)$
   if $t = int$
      $emit(\mathrm{dup})$
      $emit(\mathtt{istore}\ lookup(x))$
   else if $t = double$
      $emit(\mathrm{dup2})$
      $emit(\mathtt{dstore}\ lookup(x))$
   else
      $emit(\mathrm{dup})$
      $emit(\mathtt{astore}\ lookup(x))$

What about if the value is *not* needed? Then we can use the pop instruction,

$$\langle \mathrm{pop}, P, V, S.v \rangle \longrightarrow \langle P+1, V, S \rangle$$

and its big sister pop2. The rule is common to all uses of expressions as statements:

$compile([e : t];)$:
   $compile(e)$
   if $t \in \{int, bool, string\}$
      $emit(\mathrm{pop})$
   else if $t = double$

> $emit(\texttt{pop2})$
> **else** *return*

The last case takes case of expressions of type `void`: these leave nothing on the stack to pop. The only such expressions in our language are function calls with `void` as return type.

Declarations have a compilation scheme that emits no code, but just reserves a place in the variable storage:

> $compile(t\ x;\ ):$
> $extend(x,t)$

The extend helper function looks up the smallest available address for a variable, say i, and updates the compilation environment with the entry $(x \rightarrow i)$. The "smallest available address" is incremented by the size of the type.

Blocks are likewise compiled by creating a new part of storage, which is freed at exit from the block:

> $compile(\{s_1 \ldots s_n\}):$
> $newBlock()$
> **for** $i = 1, \ldots, n : compile(s_i)$
> $exitBlock()$

6.5   Expressions and statements with jumps

The expressions and statements of the previous section are "simple" in the sense that they are compiled into **straight code**, that is, code without **jumps**, executed in the order of instructions. Code that is not straight is needed for `if` and `while` statements but also, as we will see now, many expressions involving booleans.

The basic way to compile `while` statements is as follows:

> $compile(\texttt{while}(exp)stm):$
> $TEST := newLabel()$
> $END := newLabel()$
> $emit(TEST:)$
> $compile(exp)$
> $emit(\texttt{ifeq}\ END)$
> $compile(stm)$
> $emit(\texttt{goto}\ TEST)$
> $emit(END:)$

The generated code looks as follows, aligned with the source code statement:

```
                          TEST:
while (exp)                  exp
    stm                      ifeq END
                             stm
                             goto TEST
                          END:
```

As specified in Section 5.7, the `ifeq` instruction checks if the top of the stack is 0. If yes, the execution jumps to the label; if not, it continues to the next instruction. The checked value is the value of `exp` in the `while` condition. Value 0 means that the condition is false, hence the body is not executed. Otherwise, the value is 1 and the body `stm` is executed. After this, we take a jump back to the test of the condition.

   if statements are compiled in a similar way:

```
if (exp)                  exp
    stm1                  ifeq FALSE
else                      stm1
    stm2                  goto TRUE
                      FALSE:
                          stm2
                      TRUE:
```

The idea is to have a label for the false case, similar to the label `END` in `while` statements. But we also need a label for true, to prevent the execution of the `else` branch. The compilation scheme is straightforward to extract from this example.

   JVM has no comparison operations, conjunction, or disjunction returning boolean values. Therefore, if we want to get the value of `exp1 < exp2`, we execute code corresponding to

```
if (exp1 < exp2) 1 ; else 0 ;
```

We use the conditional jump `if_icmplt` *LABEL*, which compares the two elements on the top of the stack and jumps if the second-last is less than the last:

$$\langle \text{if\_icmplt } L, P, V, S.v.w \rangle \longrightarrow \langle P(L), V, S \rangle \ (v < w)$$
$$\langle \text{if\_icmplt } L, P, V, S.v.w \rangle \longrightarrow \langle P+1, V, S \rangle \ (v \geq w)$$

We can do this with just one label if we use code that first pushes 1 on the stack. This is overwritten by 0 if the comparison does not succeed:

```
   bipush 1
   exp1
   exp2
   if_icmplt TRUE
   pop
   bipush 0
TRUE:
```

There are instructions similar to `if_icmplt` for all comparisons of integers: `eq`, `ne`, `lt`, `gt`, `ge`, and `le`. For doubles, the mechanism is different. There is one instruction, `dcmpg`, which works as follows:

$$\langle \text{dcmpg}, P, V, S.d.e \rangle \longrightarrow \langle P+1, V, S.v \rangle$$

where $v = 1$ if $d > e$, $v = 0$ if $d = e$, and $v = -1$ if $d < e$. We leave it as an exercise (as a part of Assignment 4) to produce the full compilation schemes for both integer and double comparisons.

Putting together the compilation of comparisons and `while` loops gives terrible spaghetti code, shown in the middle column.

	`TEST:`	`TEST:`
`while (x < 9) stm`	`  bipush 1`	
	`  iload 0`	`  iload 0`
	`  bipush 9`	`  bipush 9`
	`  if_icmplt TRUE`	`  if_icmpge END`
	`  pop`	
	`  bipush 0`	
	`TRUE:`	
	`  ifeq goto END`	
	`  stm`	`  stm`
	`  goto TEST`	`  goto TEST`
	`END:`	`END:`

The right column shows better code doing the same job. It makes the comparison directly in the `while` jump, by using its *negation* `if_icmpge`; recall that `!(a < b) == (a >= b)`. The problem is: how can we get this code by using the compilation schemes?

6.6 Compositionality

A syntax-directed translation function T is **compositional**, if the value returned for a tree is a function of the values for its immediate subtrees:

$$T(Ct_1 \ldots t_n) = f(T(t_1), \ldots, T(t_n))$$

In the implementation, this means that,

- in Haskell, pattern matching does not need patterns deeper than one;

- in Java, one visitor definition per class and function is enough.

In Haskell, it would be easy to use **non-compositional** compilation schemes, by deeper patterns:

```
compile (SWhile (ELt exp1 exp2) stm) = ...
```

In Java, another visitor must be written to define what can happen depending on the condition part of `while`.

Another approach is to use compositional code generation followed by a separate phase of **back-end optimization** of the generated code: run through the code and look for code fragments that can be improved. This technique is more modular and therefore usually preferable to non-compositional hacks in code generation. We will return to optimizations in Section 6.11.

6.7   Function calls and definitions

Function calls in JVM are best understood as a generalization of arithmetic operations:

1. Push the function arguments on the stack.

2. Evaluate the function (with the arguments on the top of the stack as parameters).

3. Return the value on the stack, popping the arguments.

For instance, in function call $f(a, b, c)$, the stack evolves as follows:

S	before the call
$S.a.b.c$	entering f
$S.$	executing f, with a,b,c in variable storage
$S.v$	returning from f

The procedure is actually quite similar to what the interpreter did in Section 5.4. Entering a function `f` means that the JVM jumps to the code for `f`, with the arguments as the first available variables. The evaluation doesn't have access to old variables or to the stack of the calling code, but these become available again when the function returns.

The compilation scheme looks as follows:

$compile(f(a_1, \ldots, a_n))$:
    for $i = 1, \ldots, n$: $compile(a_i)$
    $typ := lookup(f)$
    $emit(\text{invokestatic } C/f\,typ)$

The JVM instruction for function calls is `invokestatic`. As the name suggests, we are only considering `static` methods here. The instruction needs to know the type of the function. It also needs to know its class. But we assume for simplicity that there is a global class C where all the called functions reside. The precise syntax for `invokestatic` is shown by the following example:

```
invokestatic C/mean(II)I
```

This calls a function `int mean (int x, int y)` in class C. So the type is written with a special syntax where the argument types are in parentheses before the value type. Simple types have one-letter symbols corresponding to Java types as follows:

```
I = int, D = double, V = void, Z = boolean
```

There is no difference between integers and booleans in execution, but the JVM interpreter may use the distinction for bytecode verification, that is, type checking at run time. Notice that the class, function, and type are written without spaces between in the assembly code. Complex types (corresponding to classes) have very special encodings. What we will need is

```
Ljava/lang/String; = string
```

The top level structure in JVM (as in Java) is a **class**. Function definitions are included in classes as **methods**. Here is a function and the compiled method in JVM assembler:

```
int mean (int x, int y)          .method public static mean(II)I
{                                .limit locals 2
                                 .limit stack 2
                                    iload_0
                                    iload_1
                                    iadd
                                    iconst_2
                                    idiv
  return ((x+y) / 2) ;              ireturn
}                                .end method
```

The first line obviously shows the function name and type. The function body is in the indented part. Before the body, two limits are specified: the storage needed for local variables (V in the semantic rules) and the storage needed for the evaluation stack (S in the semantics).

The local variables include the two arguments but nothing else, and since they are integers, the limit is 2. The stack can be calculated by simulating the JVM: it reaches 2 when pushing the two variables, but never beyond that. The code generator can easily calculate these limits by maintaining them in the environment; otherwise, one can use rough limits such as 1000.

Now we can give the compilation scheme for function definitions. We write $funtypeJVM(t_1, \ldots, t_m, t))$ to create the JVM representation for the type of the function.

$compile(t\ f(t_1\ x_1, \ldots, t_m\ x_m)\{s_1, \ldots, s_n\})$:
    $emit(\texttt{.method public static}\ f\ funtypeJVM(t_1, \ldots, t_m, t))$
    $emit(\texttt{.limit locals}\ locals(f))$
    $emit(\texttt{.limit stack}\ stack(f))$
    for $i = 1, \ldots, m$: $extend(x_i, t_i)$
    for $i = 1, \ldots, n$: $compile(s_i)$
    $emit(\texttt{.end method})$

We didn't show yet how to compile return statements. JVM has separate instructions for different types. Thus:

$compile(\texttt{return}\ [e : t];\ )$:
    $compile(e)$
    if $t = string$
        $emit(\texttt{areturn})$
    else if $t = double$
        $emit(\texttt{dreturn})$
    else
        $emit(\texttt{ireturn})$

$compile(\texttt{return};\ )$:
    $emit(\texttt{return})$

6.8   Putting together a class file

Class files can be built with the following template:

```
.class public Foo
.super java/lang/Object

.method public <init>()V
  aload_0
  invokenonvirtual java/lang/Object/&lt;init>()V
  return
.end method

; user's methods one by one
```

The methods are compiled as described in the previous section. Each method has its own stack, locals, and labels; in particular, a jump from one method can never reach a label in another method.

If we follow the C convention as in Chapter 5, the class must have a main method. In JVM, its type signature is different from C:

```
.method public static main([Ljava/lang/String;)V
```

following the Java convention that main takes an array of strings as its argument and returns a void. The code generator must therefore treat main as a special case: create this type signature and reserve address 0 for the array variable. The first available address for local variables is 1.

The class name, Foo in the above template, can be generated by the compiler from the file name (without suffix). The IO functions (reading and printing integers and doubles; cf. Section 5.7) can be put into a separate class, say runtime, and then called as usual:

```
invokestatic runtime/printInt(I)V
invokestatic runtime/readInt()I
```

Also a function for string concatenation (+) can be included in this class. The easiest way to produce the runtime class is to write a Java program runtime.java and compile it to runtime.class. Then you will be able to run "standard" Java code together with code generated by your own compiler.

The class file and all JVM code shown so far is not binary code but assembly code. It follows the format of **Jasmin**, which is a **JVM assembler**. In order to create the class file Foo.class, you have to compile your source code into a Jasmin file Foo.j. This is assembled by the call

```
jasmin Foo.j
```

To run your own program, write

```
java Foo
```

This executes the main function. A link for obtaining the Jasmin program is given on the book web page.

You can disassemble Java class files with the command javap -c:

```
javap -c Foo
```

The notation is slightly different from Jasmin, but this is still a good way to compare your own compiler with the standard javac compiler, and also to get hints for your own compiler. The main differences are that jumps use line numbers instead of labels, and that the ldc and invokestatic instructions refer to the runtime constant pool instead of showing explicit arguments.

6.9   Implementing code generation

In Section 6.3, we took the approach in which compilation schemes left the environment implicit, and code generation was performed by side effects. Implementing this in Java is simple as the environment can be managed by side effects, and recursive calls to the compiler in the visitor need not pass around the environment explicitly. In Haskell, however, the standard functional style would require each call to return a new environment. This was slightly awkward in the interpreter but manageable. In the compiler, however, this would make the code very messy, because the environment is so complex and needs to be changed in so many different ways.

Code generation in Haskell

Java programmers can safely skip this section.

The solution in Haskell is to use yet another monad: the **state monad**. It can be imported from the standard library `Control.Monad.State`. In the library, the type `State s v` is a monad that maintains a state of type `s` and returns a value of type `v`. Internally, it is a function of type

```
s -> (s,v)
```

which takes a state as its input and returns a value and a new state. The state can be inspected and modified by the library functions

```
get    :: State s s
modify :: (s -> s) -> State s ()
```

Following the use of *Void* in Section 6.3, we give the compilation functions a type whose return value doesn't matter:

```
compileStm :: Stm -> State Env ()
compileExp :: Stm -> State Env ()
```

Now, for instance, multiplication expressions are compiled by

```
EMul a b -> do
  compileExp a
  compileExp b
  emit $ case typExp e of
    Type_int -> imul_Instr
    Type_double -> dmul_Instr
```

The helper function `typExp` is easy to define if the type checker has type-annotated all trees, as explained in Section 4.10.

The environment has several components: symbol tables for functions and variables, counters for variable addresses and labels, and also a counter for the maximum stack depth if you want to give an accurate figure to `limit stack` (Section 6.7). But the definition above assumes that also the code is put into the environment! Otherwise both recursive calls to `compileExp` would need to return some code, and the last step would concatenate these pieces with the multiplication instruction.

Here is a partial definition of the environment, only containing what is needed for variables and the code:

```
data Env = Env [
  vars      :: [Map Ident Int],
  maxvar    :: Int,
  code      :: [Instruction]
  }
```

The `emit` function works by changing the `code` part of the environment with the state monad library function `modify` (notice that the instructions are collected in reverse order, which is more efficient):

```
emit :: Instruction -> State Env ()
emit i c = modify (\s -> s{code = i : code s})
```

Similarly, the lookup of a variable address uses the `get` function for state monads:

```
lookupVar :: Ident -> State Env Int
lookupVar x = do
  s <- get
  -- then look up the first occurrence of x in (vars s)
```

Notice that a stack (i.e. list) of variable environments is needed, to take care of block structure.

All operations of Section 6.3 can be implemented in a state monad by using the `get` and `modify` functions, so that the imperative flavour and simplicity of the compilation schemes is preserved.

Code generation in Java

Haskell programmers can safely skip this section.

We use a `CodeGenerator` class similar to the `TypeChecker` class in Chapter 4 and the `Interpreter` class in Chapter 5, with a visitor taking care of syntax-directed translation. The environment must be adapted to the needs of code generation, as specified in Section 6.3. Moreover, we now declare an environment as a class variable in CodeGenerator, so that we can access it by side effects in the compilation methods. Thus we don't pass around an Env argument, but just a dummy Object. We could of course do the same in the type checker and the interpreter as well—the main reason why we didn't was to keep the Java code as close to the abstract specification as possible. By the same argument, we now hide the environment.

Here is a part of the Java class which, just like the Haskell code in the previous section, shows the main type signatures and the implementation of multiplication and a simplified Env class. Code generation is done by simply printing the instructions as strings. However, you can also collect the code in env and output it later. In this way, you can easily compute the maximum stack depth in env and emit an accurate stack limit before emitting the code.

```
public class CodeGenerator {

  public void compile(Program p)

  private static class Env {
    private LinkedList<HashMap<String,Integer>> vars;
    private Integer maxvar;

    public Env() {
      vars = new LinkedList<HashMap<String,Integer>>();
      maxvar = 0 ;
    }
    public void addVar(String x, TypeCode t) {
    // use TypeCode to determine the increment of maxvar
    }
  }

  private Env env = new Env() ;

  private void compileStm(Stm st, Object arg) {
    st.accept(new StmCompiler(), arg);
  }

  private class StmCompiler implements Stm.Visitor<Object,Object> {
    public Object visit(Mini.Absyn.SDecl p, Object arg) {
      env.addVar(p.ident_, typeCode(p.type));
      return null;
    }
```

```
  }

  private Object compileExp(Exp e, Object arg) {
    return e.accept(new ExpCompiler(), arg);
  }

  private class ExpCompiler implements Exp.Visitor<Object,Object> {
    public Object visit(Mini.Absyn.EMul p, Object arg) {
      p.exp_1.accept(this, arg) ;
      p.exp_2.accept(this, arg) ;
      if (typeCodeExp(p.exp_1) == TypeCode.INT) {
        System.err.println("imul");
        } else {
        System.err.println("dmul");
        }
      return null ;
    }
  }
}
```

Notice the need of type information in the compilation of EMul. This information is assumed to be obtained from the expression. The best way to do this is to let the type checker annotate all expressions with types, as explained in Section 4.10.

6.10 Compiling to native code*

Native code means the machine language of a real processor, such as the **Intel x86** series. This series dates back to the 8086 processor from 1978. Later members of the family include 8088 (the **IBM PC**), 80286, 80386, and the Pentium. These processors have remained backward compatible to a set of instructions, which has only been grown and not shrunken. These processors are used in almost all desktop and laptop computers of today, with Linux, Mac OS, and Windows alike. Therefore their machine language provides the easiest way to experiment with native code compilation.

The main difference between x86 and JVM is that x86 has **registers**. Registers are places for data in the processor itself (as opposed to the memory), and they can be accessed immediately by for instance arithmetic operations. For example,

```
add eax, ebx
```

is an instruction to add the value of the register **ebx** to the value in **eax**. Thus it corresponds to an assignment

```
eax := eax + ebx
```

The notation we will use is that of the assembly language **NASM, Netwide Assembler**. NASM has open-source freely available tools and documentation; see Appendix D for further information.

The machine also has a notion of a **stack**; it is a part of the memory that can be accessed by its address. A memory address consists of a register (which usually marks the start of the currently available memory segment) with an **offset**, that is, the distance of the address from the register value as the number of bytes. Thus for instance

```
add eax, [ebp-8]
```

means an addition to `eax` of the value stored in the address `[ebp-8]`, where `ebp` is the register pointing to the beginning of the current **stack frame**, that is, the memory segment available for the current function call.

Let us look at a little example: a function computing the Fibonacci numbers less than 500. We write the source code and corresponding NASM code side by side.

```
int fib ()               fib:
{                            enter 0,0      ; prepare stack frame
  int hi,lo ;                ; reserve eax for hi, ebx for lo
  hi = 1 ;                   mov eax, 1     ; eax := 1
  lo = hi ;                  mov ebx, eax   ; ebx := eax
  printInt(hi) ;             call printInt  ; print eax
  while (hi < 500) { test:
                             cmp eax, 500   ; set values to compare
                             jge end        ; jump if eax >= 500
    printInt(hi) ;           call printInt
    hi = hi + lo ;           add eax, ebx   ; eax := eax + ebx
    lo = hi - lo ;           mov ecx, eax   ; ecx := eax temporarily
                             sub ecx, ebx   ; ecx := ecx - ebx
                             mov ebx, ecx   ; ebx := ecx
                             jmp test       ; jump back to test
  }                        end:
  return 0 ;                 mov eax, 0     ; return value
                             leave          ; leave stack frame
}                            ret            ; return to caller
```

The structure of the code is somewhat similar to JVM, in particular the way the `while` loop is expressed with labels and jumps. The arithmetic operations potentially need fewer instructions than in JVM; notice, however, that we use three instructions and a temporary register `ecx` for the subtraction `lo = hi - lo`, because it is not of the directly translatable form *dest := dest op src*.

There are very few registers available in x86 for integers. Any number of them may be needed as temporaries when evaluating expressions. Therefore a compiler cannot usually reserve registers for variables, but they are stored in memory, and the code becomes less efficient than the idealized hand-written code shown above. An optimizing compiler can improve the code by **register allocation**, as will be explained in Section 6.11.

Another difference from JVM is in the way functions are compiled. JVM was designed for object-oriented programs, and it has an inherent structure of classes and methods corresponding to the structure of Java programs. In x86, there is no such structure, but just code loosely grouped by labels. Thus the start of the function `fib` is marked with the same kind of label as is used for the `while` loop. This means more freedom for the assembly programmer and the compiler writer.

As a compiler must work for all possible input in a systematic way, it must follow some discipline of **calling conventions**: the way in which arguments are passed and values are returned. In JVM, the calling convention is fixed: the arguments are pushed on the stack when entering a function, and popped when the function returns and leaves just the value on the stack. In x86, this is just one possible convention to follow: one can also use registers. For instance, the Fibonacci code above uses `eax` for the return value of `fib`, but also for passing the argument to `printInt`. We carefully chose it also to store the variable `hi` in `eax`, because `hi` was the argument always passed to `printInt`. In this way we saved many copying (`mov`) instructions. But in general, a compiler cannot assume such lucky coincidences.

To get a flavour of calling conventions, let us consider the ones normally used in compiling C programs. Just like in JVM, a stack is used. The stack contains both the local variables and the temporary values of evaluation; unlike in JVM, some of these may be held in registers instead of the stack. Each function call has its own part of the stack, known as its **stack frame**. The address of the beginning of the stack frame is stored in the **frame pointer**, for which the register `ebp` is used. Another register, `esp`, is used as the **stack pointer**, which points to the current top of the stack. When a function *new* is called from within *old*, the following steps are performed:

1. Push values of the registers on the stack (to save them).

2. Push the arguments in reverse order.

3. Push the **return address** (i.e. code pointer back to *old*).

4. Push the frame pointer value of *old* (to save it).

5. Use the old stack pointer as frame pointer of *new*.

6. Reserve stack space for the local variables of *new*.

7. Execute the code of *new*.

8. Return the value of *new* in register `eax`.

9. Restore the *old* frame pointer value.

10. Jump to the saved return address.

11. Restore the values of saved registers.

Notice the importance of saving registers before calling a function. Every function uses registers in its own way and does not know what other functions might have called it and how they use the registers. But since every function has its own part of the stack (its stack frame), values stored on the stack are safe. Either the caller or the callee (i.e. the called function) must make sure to save registers on the stack; in the steps above, the caller does this.

Also notice the saving of the return address. Again, the callee cannot know where it has been called from. But the caller has saved the pointer to the calling code, and the execution of the program can continue from there when the callee has returned. In JVM, this is not visible in the code, because the JVM interpreter uses a hard-coded way of calling functions, which includes keeping track of return addresses.

To give an example, let us look at the functions

```
old(x,y) { ... new(e) ... }
new(x)   { ... }
```

in a situation where `old` has called `new`. When the call of `new` is active, the stack looks as shown in Figure 6.1.

We follow the convention of drawing the stack so that it grows downwards. This reflects the way memory addresses are created: the offsets are positive before the frame pointer, negative after it. Thus, for instance, inside `old` before calling `new`,

- the saved frame pointer is in `[ebp+4]`,

- the return address is in `[ebp+8]`,

- the first argument is `[ebp+12]`,

- the second argument is `[ebp+16]`;

- the first local variable is `[ebp]`,

- the second local variable is `[ebp-4]`.

⋮	local variables of the caller of `old`
⋮	saved registers of the caller of old
2	second argument to `old`
1	first argument to `old`
ret	saved return address for the call of `old`
fp	saved frame pointer of the caller of `old`
_____	← frame pointer of `old`
⋮	local variables of `old`
⋮	saved registers of `old`
3	argument to `new`
ret	saved return address for the call of `new`
fp	saved frame pointer of `old`
_____	← frame pointer of `new`
⋮	local variables of `new`
	← stack pointer

Figure 6.1: Stack at point i in call `old(1,2){...new(3){...i...}...}`.

- the third local variable is `[ebp-8]`.

assuming the arguments and variables are integers and consume 4 bytes each.

The C-style calling conventions are supported by some special instructions: `enter` for entering a stack frame, `leave` for leaving a stack frame, `pusha` for pushing certain registers to the stack to save them, and `popa` for popping the values back to the same registers. Instructions like these make the assembly code shorter, but they may consume more processor time than the simpler instructions. One of the problems of x86 compilation is indeed the selection of instructions, due to its **CISC** architecture (**Complex Instruction Set Computing**). Another complicating feature of x86 is that floating point operations work in a way rather different from the (historically older) integer operations.

One solution to the complications is the **RISC** architecture (**Reduced Instruction Set Computing**), whose most common current appearance is in the **ARM processor** used in mobile phones. RISC machines have fewer instructions than x86, and these instructions are simpler and more uniform. They also tend to have more registers, which work in a more uniform way.

But a more radical solution to native code compilation is to do it via intermediate code, such as **LLVM** (derived from "Low Level Virtual Machine", which is no longer its official name). LLVM has a RISC-style instruction set with an infinite supply of **virtual registers**. Compilers can just generate

LLVM code and leave the generation of native code to LLVM tools.

Exercise 6-0. Compile the above Fibonacci program to assembly code with GCC, by the command

```
gcc -S fib.c
```

and try to understand the resulting file `fib.s`. The code is not NASM, but this is probably not the main problem. You can use the standard library function call `printf("%i\n",hi)` to express `printInt(hi)`, if you put `#include <stdio.h>` in the beginning of the file.

Exercise 6-1. Write compilation schemes for integer constants, variables, additions, subtractions, an multiplications in NASM. Assume the availability of four integer registers (eax, ebx, ecx, edx) and an unlimited supply of stack memory in addresses [ebp-4k] (that is, the offsets are multiples of 4). The arithmetic instructions have the syntax

$$(\texttt{add}|\texttt{sub}|\texttt{imul}|\texttt{mov})\ dest,\ src$$

with the effect of changing *dest* by the addition, subtraction, or multiplication with *src*; `mov` just copies *src* to *dest*. The *source src* and the *destination dest* are registers or memory addresses, but at most one of them may be a memory address! The source can also be an **immediate value**, that is, an integer constant.

Before tackling the compilation itself, write by hand the target code for the expression

```
(x + y + z) * 2 + (y + z + u + v) * 3 - (u + v + w) * 4
```

Also use this as a test case for your compilation schemes. If you want to test your compiler in reality, the book *PC Assembly Language* by Paul Carter gives you the information needed (see Appendix D).

6.11   Code optimization*

Optimizations are an important part of modern compilers. A naïve user might expect them to do some magic that turns badly written source code into efficient machine code. However, this is not the usual purpose of optimizations. The main purpose is, actually, just to tidy up the mess that earlier compilation phases have created! This is a part of the modular way of thinking in modern compiler construction. Each compilation phase (Section 1.4) should be as simple as possible, so that it can be understood clearly and reused in different combinations. If a phase threatens to become too complex, it gets split into separate phases. We have already looked at two such cases: instruction selection, which we wanted to perform in a compositional way (Section 6.6), and register allocation, which is also better postponed to a phase after code generation (Section 6.10).

Of course, the purpose of optimization can also be to improve the code written by the programmer. It is then typically used for encouraging high-level ways of programming—to free the programmer from thinking about low-level details that can be left to the machine. One example is the technique of **constant folding**. It allows the user to write statements such as

```
int age = 26 * 365 + 7 * 366 + 31 + 28 + 4 ;
```

which says much more and is easier to write than

```
int age = 12115 ;
```

Constant folding means that operations on constants are carried out at compile time. Thus the shown complex expression will only consume one push instruction in the JVM.

Constant folding can be seen as a special case of a technique known as **partial evaluation**. It means the evaluation of expressions at compile time, which in general is not total, because some variables get their values only at run time. It needs a lot of care. For example, a tempting rule of partial evaluation could be to reduce all self-subtractions into zero,

$$e - e \Longrightarrow 0$$

But this can go wrong in several ways. One is the situation where e has side effects—for instance,

```
i++ - i++
```

or a function call f() which returns an integer but prints hello each time.

Pure languages are ones in which expression evaluation doesn't have side effects. The advantage is that they can be optimized more aggressively than non-pure languages—in fact, this is just one example of the ease of **reasoning about code** in pure languages. Haskell is an example of a language that is, at least almost, pure, and enjoys strongly optimizing compilers, such as GHC. But even in pure languages, care is needed—for instance, the expression

```
1/x - 1/x
```

cannot be optimized to 0, because this would change the computation in the case where x is 0 and raises a run-time exception.

Another technique used for improving source programs is **tail recursion elimination**. A function is tail recursive if the last thing it does is call itself:

$$f(\ldots)\{\ldots f(\ldots);\}$$

The normal, unoptimized compilation of functions creates new stack frames for each call. It is not uncommon that a recursive function calls itself, say, a hundred times before it finally returns. If each stack frame needs a thousand bytes of space, then the recursion needs hundred thousand bytes. In a tail recursive function, this is unnecessary: instead of building a new stack frame, the function can just re-run and update the variables of the old stack frame in place. Tail recursion elimination is used both in imperative and functional languages, for instance, in GCC. Its purpose is to encourage programmers to write recursive functions, which is considered good programming style.

Let us conclude with a couple of optimization techniques used in the compiler pipeline, to clean up the results of quick and simple earlier phases. These techniques are applied to the machine code or, even better, to intermediate code such as LLVM.

Peephole optimization is a procedure that goes through the code and looks for segments that could be improved. The segments typically have a limited size—the size of the peephole. For instance, a peephole optimizer with size 3 for JVM could implement constant folding as follows:

```
bipush 5
bipush 6          bipush 5
bipush 7   ⟹     bipush 42   ⟹    bipush 47
imul              iadd
iadd
```

This example also shows that iterating the process can result in more optimizations, because the eliminable addition expression has here been created by first eliminating the multiplication. Another example is the elimination of stack duplication for an assignment whose value is not needed (cf. Section 6.4):

```
                  bipush 6
i = 6 ;   ⟶      dup         ⟹    bipush 6
                  istore 4           istore 4
                  pop
```

The natural implementation of peephole optimization is by pattern matching over instruction sequences. Having a large peephole may lead to complex patterns, which slow down the process. This is an example of the typical trade-off between time needed for compilation and the savings gained for run-time programs.

Register allocation is a procedure that tries to fit all variables and temporary values of a program to a given set of registers. The small set of registers in x86 is an example. This task is usually performed on an intermediate language such as LLVM, after first letting the code generator use an unlimited supply of registers, known as **virtual registers**.

The main concept in register allocation is **liveness**: variables that are "live" at the same time cannot be kept in the same register. Live means that the value of the variable may be needed later in the program. Here is an example piece of code with the liveness of variables marked beside each statement:

```
int x = 1 ;          // x      live
int y = 2 ;          // x y    live
printInt(y) ;        // x      live
int z = 3 ;          // x    z live
printInt(x + z) ; // x    z live
y = z - x ;          //    y   live
z = f(y) ;           //    y   live
printInt(y) ;
return ;
```

How many registers are needed for the three variables x, y, and z? The answer is two, because y and z are never live at the same time and can hence be kept in the same register.

A classic algorithm for register allocation works in two steps:

1. **Liveness analysis**: find out which variables are live at the same time, to define an **interference graph**, where the nodes are variables and edges express the relation "live at the same time".

2. **Graph colouring**: colour the nodes of the graph so that the same colour can be used for two nodes if they are not connected.

The colours in the second step correspond to registers. The example program above has the following interference graph:

It shows that y and z can be given the same colour. Graph colouring is of course a very general algorithm. It is also used for colouring countries on a map, where the "interference" of two countries means that they have a common border.

Liveness analysis is an example of a family of techniques known as **dataflow analysis**. In addition to register allocation, it can be used for tasks such as **dead-code elimination**: a piece of code is dead if it can never be reached when running a program. For example, an assignment to a variable that is not live is dead code; z = f(y) in the code above is a case in point. However, caution is needed even here, because f(y) may have to be executed for side effects.

In general, finding the "optimal" code for a given program is an undecidable problem. For instance, in a conditional statement

if (condition) then_branch else else_branch

the *else_branch* part is dead code if *condition* is uniformly true. But *condition* may well express an undecidable proposition, even if it doesn't depend on run-time variables.

Exercise 6-2. Experiment with gcc and javac to find out which optimizations they perform. Unlike javac, gcc has different **optimization levels**, which can be set by flags such as -O2.

Exercise 6-3. Give examples of undecidable conditions, both with and without variables that are only known at run time.

Exercise 6-4. **Simplify and select graph colouring** works in the following way: to colour a graph with k colours,

1. Take away any node with less than k edges, together with its edges, until no nodes are left. Maintain a list (a stack) of the removed nodes and their edges when they are removed.

2. When the graph is empty, rebuild it starting from the top of the stack (i.e. from the last node removed). Since every node in the stack has less than k neighbours, each node can always be given a colour that is different from its neighbours.

Of course, the procedure need not work for all graphs and all numbers k, since it may be the case that every node has k or more neighbours. But you can test this algorithm first with the simple graph shown above and 2 colours. Then with a non-trivial example: draw a map of continental Europe and try to colour it with 4 colours. Germany, for instance, has 9 neighbours, and its neighbour Austria has 8. But you should start with the countries with less neighbours and hope that at every point there will be countries with less than 4 neighbours left.

Chapter 7

Functional Programming Languages

The previous chapters have mostly concerned the implementation of imperative languages. This chapter takes a look at a new, fascinating world, where the language is much simpler but in many ways more powerful. If the grammar for the C++ fragment treated before was 50 lines, a useful functional language can be defined on less than 15 lines. But the simplicity is more on the user's side than the compiler writer's: you are likely to bang your head against the wall a few times, until you get it right with recursion, call by name, and closures—not to mention polymorphic type checking, which is presented as optional material. The work is helped by a rigorous and simple rule system; more than ever before, you need your discipline and perseverance to render it correctly in implementation code.

This chapter provides all the concepts and tools needed for solving Assignment 5, which is an interpreter for a fragment of Haskell.

7.1   Programming paradigms

There are thousands of programming languages, but they all fit into a few **programming language paradigms**, that is, ways of thinking about programming. In the **imperative paradigm**, also known as **procedural**, a program is a series of **statements** that affect a **state**. The state was called **environment** in Chapter 5, and contains the values of variables. In the **functional paradigm**, executing a program is, simply, evaluating an expression; no state is needed.

With this characterization, it sounds like imperative programming is more general than functional programming, because imperative programs also evaluate expressions. It sounds like functional programming only uses a subset of the program constructs that imperative programs use. And this is actually true: the level of statements is missing. A source file for a functional program consists of function definitions, just like a source file for an imperative program. But a function definition is simply a definition of an expression with variables.

Here is an example of a functional program, which could be written in Haskell but actually also in the language that we are going to implement in Assignment 5:

```
doub x     = x + x ;
twice f x = f (f x) ;
quadruple = twice doub ;
main       = twice quadruple 2 ;
```

This program has four function definitions. The first one defines a function called `doub`, which for its argument x returns $x + x$. The second one defines `twice`, which iterates the application of a function on an argument twice. The third one, `quadruple`, applies `twice` to `doub`. The fourth one, `main`, prints the result of applying `twice` to `quadruple` and 2.

We will explain the syntax and semantics of our functional language more properly soon. Just one thing is needed now: we follow the syntax of Haskell and write function applications by just putting the function and its arguments one after the other,

$$f\,x\,y\,z$$

whereas languages like C, and also ordinary mathematics, use parentheses and commas,

$$f(x, y, z)$$

As we will see later, this simplified notation is actually very logical. But let us first walk through the computation of `main` in the above example:

```
  main
= twice quadruple 2
= quadruple (quadruple 2)
= twice doub (twice doub 2)
= doub (doub (doub (doub 2)))
= doub (doub (doub (2 + 2)))
= doub (doub (doub 4))
= doub (doub (4 + 4))
= doub (doub 8)
= doub (8 + 8)
= doub 16
= 16 + 16
= 32
```

What we do in each step is replace some part of the expression by its definition, possibly also replacing variables by their actual arguments. This operation is called **substitution**, and it could be defined with syntax-directed translation. However, it is very tricky in the presence of variable bindings and also computationally expensive. Therefore we will use a better method when building an interpreter in Section 7.4, generalizing the interpreter of function calls in imperative languages (Section 5.4).

7.2 Functions as values

Evaluating expressions and defining functions is not unique to functional programming. For instance, the doub function can be defined in C and Java as well:

```
// doub x    = x + x

int doub (int x)
{
  return x + x ;
}
```

But this mechanism is restricted to what is called **first-order functions**: the arguments are objects like numbers and class objects—but not themselves functions.

In C++, it is also possible to write **second-order functions**, which take functions as arguments. This is what we need for the twice function:

```
// twice f x = f (f x)

int twice(int f (int n), int x)
{
  return f(f(x)) ;
}
```

In a functional language, functions are **first-class citizens**. This means that a function has a value even if it is not applied. And this is why functions can return functions and take functions as arguments. As shown by twice, functions in C++ have the status of first-class citizens when used as arguments. But they are still not quite first-class, because we cannot *return* a function as a value. Thus we cannot define exactly as in Haskell:

```
// quadruple = twice doub
```

```
// not possible:
(int f (int x)) quadruple()
{
  return twice(doub) ;
}
```

What we must do is pass an additional argument, which enables `quadruple` to return an integer and not a function:

```
int quadruple(int x)
{
  return twice(doub, x) ;
}
```

This corresponds to another definition in Haskell:

```
quadruple x = twice doub x
```

This definition has the same meaning as the one without x; hence adding or removing the second variable doesn't change the meaning of the function.

To understand what precisely happens in function definitions, we introduce types for functions. In Haskell-like languages, they are written in the following way:

```
max : Int -> Int -> Int
```

(Haskell uses a double colon `::` for typing, but we stick to a single `:`.) The notation is right-associative, and hence equivalent to

```
max : Int -> (Int -> Int)
```

The typing rule for function applications is:

$$\frac{\Gamma \vdash f : A \to B \quad \Gamma \vdash a : A}{\Gamma \vdash f a : B}$$

Thus **partial application** is meaningful: we have a valid typing

```
max 4 : Int -> Int
```

This is a function that returns the maximum of its argument and 4. Notice that application is left-associative, with `max 4 5` the same as `(max 4) 5`.

In many other languages, the value of a function must be a "basic type", i.e. not a function type. This corresponds to having a **tuple** of arguments:

```
maxt : (Int * Int) -> Int
```

Tuples are a type of its own, which has the following typing rule:

$$\frac{\Gamma \vdash a : A \quad \Gamma \vdash b : B}{\Gamma \vdash (a, b) : A * B}$$

Partial application cannot access parts of tuples. Hence, using a function over a tuple forces its application to both arguments.

But there is an equivalence between functions over tuples and two-place functions:

$$(A * B) \to C \iff A \to B \to C$$

Converting the first to the second is called **currying**, with reference to Haskell B. Curry, the logician who invented many of the ideas underlying functional programming. It is a powerful programming technique, but it also simplifies the semantics and implementation of programming languages; for instance, as we have seen, it enables the encoding of many-place functions as one-place functions, which simplifies both the type checking and interpretation rules.

7.3 Anonymous functions

In imperative languages, functions only exist when someone has defined them, and they can only be accessed by the names given in those definitions. In a functional language, you can also form **anonymous functions**, by taking apart a variable from an expression with an expression form called **lambda abstraction**:

```
timesNine = twice (\x -> x + x + x)
```

Syntactically, a **lambda abstract** is an expression

$$\lambda x.e$$

formed from a variable x and an expression e. Following Haskell's notation, the Greek letter λ is in programming language code replaced by the ASCII symbol \ (backslash), and the dot (.) by the ASCII arrow ->. A verbal expression for the lambda abstract is, "function which for x returns e". Thus, for instance, \x -> x + x + x is a function that for the argument x returns $x + x + x$.

The typing rule for lambda abstracts is the following:

$$\frac{\Gamma, x : A \vdash e : B}{\Gamma \vdash \lambda x.e : A \to B}$$

Thus lambda abstraction is a way to build functions. Actually, it is the only way that is really needed, because a function definition

$$f\, x_1\, \ldots\, x_n = e$$

can be expressed as the definition of a constant f as a lambda abstract,

$$f = \lambda x_1. \ldots \lambda x_n.e$$

This leads to a further simplification of the language and its implementation: the environment can contain simply identifiers and their types (in the type checker) or values (in the interpreter).

In C++, we cannot write `timesNine` in the same direct way, but have to define a named tripling function first:

```
// triple x = x + x + x
int triple(int x)
{
   return x + x + x ;
}

// timesNine = twice triple
int timesNine(int x)
{
   return twice(triple, x) ;
}
```

But there is an experimental **Lambda Library** in C++ permitting anonymous functions.

7.4   Evaluating expressions

A functional language can be very useful with an extremely small core. We start with a language with only four expression forms:

```
Exp  ::=
    Ident                        -- variables, constants
  | Integer                      -- integer literals
  | "(" "\" Ident "->" Exp ")"   -- abstractions
  | "(" Exp Exp ")"              -- applications
```

The operational semantics uses judgements of the usual form,

$$\gamma \vdash e \Downarrow v$$

which is read, "in the environment γ, the expression e evaluates to the value v". Notice that evaluation cannot change the environment. This is because we are dealing with a **purely functional language**, a language without side effects.

As in Chapter 5, the environment is a set of values assigned to variables, which we denote by

$$x := v,\ y := w, \ldots$$

As **values**, however, we have to be much more general than in the imperative language, because values are not only numbers and other simple objects, but also complex objects—in particular, functions. In a first version of the semantics, we could simply assume that *values are expressions*. Evaluation is then a procedure that converts an expression to another expression. This other expression is often simpler than the first expression, as in

$$2 + 3 * 8 \Downarrow 26$$

But it can also be more complex. For instance, the Haskell function `replicate` creates a list of some number of copies of an object, so that for instance

```
replicate 20 1 ⇓ [1,1,1,1,1,1,1,1,1,1,1,1,1,1,1,1,1,1,1,1]
```

A value, in general terms, is the expected end result of a computation—the point from which the evaluation cannot proceed further. Thus clearly 2 + 3 * 8 is not a value, because the evaluation can proceed by performing multiplication and addition. On the other hand, in many occasions $2^{31} - 1$ is much more interesting as a value than 2147483647, because it is more informative for the human observer.

But is 2 + 3 * x a value? In one sense, it is: we cannot take it any further, because we don't known what x is. In another sense, it isn't: we were expecting to get a number, but we don't have one yet. The way to get one is by first giving a value to x and then performing multiplication and addition.

Whatever expressions count as values, they must *not* contain variables. More accurately, they must not contain **free variables**. A free variable is a variable that is not **bound**, and being bound means that there is a lambda binding. The precise definition is by syntax-directed translation, defining the set *free* of the free variables of an expression:

$$free(x) = \{x\}$$
$$free(i) = \{\}$$
$$free(f\ a) = free(f) \cup free(a)$$
$$free(\lambda x.b) = free(b) - \{x\}$$

An expression that has no free variables (i.e. $free(e) = \{\}$) is a **closed expression**. An expression that does have free variables is an **open expression**. The definition of `free` implies that the closed expressions are those where all variables are bound by lambdas. This includes as a special case those expressions that have no variables.

As an approximation of what values are we could now say: values are closed expressions. In practice, however, it is better to include yet another ingredient: to allow open expressions together with values for their free variables. For instance,

```
(2 + 3 * x){x := 8}
```

is such a value. It could be computed further, by replacing x with 8. But we can regard this as good enough a value even without further computation.

In general terms, we will use values of the form

$$e\{\gamma\}$$

where e is an expression and γ is an environment. The environment gives values to the free variables of the expression. It so to speak *closes* the expression, and is therefore called a **closure**.

The semantics we are now going to formulate uses two kinds of values:

- integers

- closures of lambda abstracts

The rules for variables and integer literals are simple: a variable expression is evaluated by looking up the variable in the environment.

$$\frac{}{\gamma \vdash x \Downarrow v} \quad x := v \text{ is in } \gamma$$

An integer literal evaluates to itself.

$$\gamma \vdash i \Downarrow i$$

For lambda abstracts, the normal procedure is: do nothing. A lambda abstract is itself a perfect representation of a function as a value. However, the body of the lambda abstract may contain some other variables than the one bound by the lambda. These variables get their values in the evaluation environment, which is therefore added to the expression to form a closure:

$$\gamma \vdash (\lambda x.e) \Downarrow (\lambda x.e)\{\gamma\}$$

Function application is the most complex case. Here we can recall how we did for the imperative language in Section 5.4. There we had to deal with applications to many arguments simultaneously, whereas here it is enough to consider functions with one argument. Recalling moreover that evaluation has no side effects, we can consider the following special case of the application rule:

$$\frac{\gamma \vdash a \Downarrow u \quad x := u \vdash s_1 \ldots s_n \Downarrow v}{\gamma \vdash f(a) \Downarrow v} \quad \text{if } V \ f(T\,x)\{s_1 \ldots s_n\} \text{ in } \gamma$$

Adapting this rule to the functional language requires two changes:

- The function body: in the imperative language, it is a sequence of statements, $s_1 \ldots s_n$; in the functional language, it is a lambda abstraction body e, which is an expression.

- The function f: in the imperative language, it is always an explicitly defined function symbol; in the functional language, it can be any expression (for instance, a lambda abstract or an application).

The latter difference implies that the evaluation of f is not simply a look-up in the function table. But we can just replace the look-up by a step of evaluating the expression f. This evaluation results in a closure, with a lambda abstract $\lambda x.e$ and an environment δ. Then $(f\,a)$ is computed by evaluating e in an environment where the variable x is set to the value of the argument a:

$$\frac{\gamma \vdash f \Downarrow (\lambda x.e)\{\delta\} \quad \gamma \vdash a \Downarrow u \quad \delta, x := u \vdash e \Downarrow v}{\gamma \vdash (f\,a) \Downarrow v}$$

To show how this works in practice, assume the function definition

```
doub x = x + x
```

which means the same as

```
doub = \x -> x + x
```

Now we can compute doub 4 as follows:

$$\frac{\vdash \mathbf{doub} \Downarrow (\lambda x.x + x)\{\} \quad \vdash 4 \Downarrow 4 \quad x := 4 \vdash x + x \Downarrow 8}{\vdash (\mathbf{doub}\,4) \Downarrow 8}$$

In this case, the applied function has no free variables. But this is just a limiting case. The need of closures is shown by an example with a two-place function,

```
plus x y = x + y
```

Here is the evaluation of the expression plus 3 4 (i.e. ((plus 3) 4)):

$$\frac{\dfrac{\vdash \mathbf{plus} \Downarrow (\lambda x.\lambda y.x + y)\{\} \quad \vdash 3 \Downarrow 3 \quad x := 3 \vdash (\lambda y.x + y) \Downarrow (\lambda y.x + y)\{x := 3\}}{\vdash (\mathbf{plus}\,3) \Downarrow (\lambda y.x + y)\{x := 3\}} \quad \vdash 4 \Downarrow 4 \quad x := 3, y := 4 \vdash x + y \Downarrow 7}{\vdash ((\mathbf{plus}\,3)\,4) \Downarrow 7}$$

7.5 Call by value vs. call by name

In Section 5.5, we noted that function application is usually implemented by the **call by value** strategy. This was also used in the application rule shown in the previous section: the argument is evaluated first, before evaluating the body. In the **call by name** strategy, the argument is passed unevaluated to the body. This strategy is equally easy to implement: the application rule now becomes

$$\frac{\gamma \vdash f \Downarrow (\lambda x \to e)\{\delta\} \quad \delta, x := a\{\gamma\} \vdash e \Downarrow v}{\gamma \vdash (f\,a) \Downarrow v}$$

Notice that the expression a alone would not work as the value of x. It is not a value but an expression, and hence needs to be made into a closure. The proper way to close it is to use γ, because this is the environment in which a would be evaluated if we were performing call by value.

All the difference between the two strategies thus results from a very small difference in the rule for function application; all the other rules remain the same. But the consequences are significant. Let us consider the following program:

```
infinite = 1 + infinite
first x y = x
main = first 5 infinite
```

With call by value, we get

```
main
= first 5 infinite
= (\x -> \y -> x) 5 (1 + infinite)
= (\y -> 5) (1 + infinite)
= (\y -> 5) (2 + infinite)
...
```

which leads to non-termination. Even though the function `first` ignores its second argument, call-by-value requires this argument to be evaluated.

With call by name,

```
main
= first 5 infinite
= (\x -> \y -> x) 5 infinite
= (\y -> 5) infinite
= 5
```

There is no attempt to evaluate the second argument, because it is not needed by `first`.

In general, there can be many different orders of evaluation for an expression, depending on what parts are evaluated first. Some orders may terminate while some others may loop. Call-by-value and call-by-name are just two possible orders. But call-by-name has the property that it is "the most terminating" one: if there is *any* order that makes the evaluation of an expression terminate, then call-by-name is such an order.

Why isn't call by name always used then? The reason is that it may be less efficient, since it may lead to some expressions getting evaluated many times, i.e. once for each time the argument is used. With call by value, the expression is evaluated just once, and its value is then reused for all occurrences of the variable. The following pair of examples shows what happens:

```
doub x = x + x

doub (doub 8)
= doub 8 + doub 8   -- by name
= 8 + 8 + 8 + 8
= 32

doub (doub 8)
= doub 16          -- by value
= 16 + 16
= 32
```

Haskell is a language that uses an intermediate strategy, **call by need**. In this strategy, the expression is not evaluated when it is put to the environment, which is similar to call by name. But when the value is needed for the first time, the result of evaluation is saved in the environment, and the next look-up of the variable will not need to compute it again.

7.6 Implementing an interpreter

Let us now build an interpreter. We will work with a slightly extended language, to make it interesting to use in practice. The language has two more forms of expressions: infix operations and if-then-else. With usual precedences, we get the following BNF grammar:

```
Exp3 ::= Ident
Exp3 ::= Integer
Exp2 ::= Exp2 Exp3
Exp1 ::= Exp1 "+" Exp2
Exp1 ::= Exp1 "-" Exp2
Exp1 ::= Exp1 "<" Exp2
Exp  ::= "if" Exp1 "then" Exp1 "else" Exp
Exp  ::= "\\" Ident "->" Exp
```

A program in the language is a sequence of function definitions, each of which has the form

$$f\, x_1 \ldots x_n = e\,;$$

Here is an example program:

```
doub x = x + x ;
pow x = if (x < 1) then 1 else doub (pow (x-1)) ;
main = pow 30 ;
```

The function pow defines powers of 2 by recursion.

The execution of programs is defined in the same way as in the imperative case (Section 5.6): evaluate the expression main. The evaluation is carried out in an environment consisting of all functions mapped to their definitions. Each definition looks like a closure, which contains the defining expression and an empty environment. For instance, the example program above creates the following environment:

```
doub := (\x -> x + x){}
pow  := (\x -> if (x < 1) then 1 else doub (pow (x-1))){}
main := (pow 30){}
```

We have written {} to mark the empty variable list, to make it clear that the values are closures and not expressions.

Just like in Chapter 5, the environment should be divided to two parts: the top-level function symbols and the local variables (which always result from lambdas). This might first look unnecessary, because the syntax doesn't make a distinction between function symbols and variables. However, we want to avoid carrying around all functions whenever we build closures. Closures with all functions would be too heavy. What is even worse, they would be impossible when recursive functions are present. It is enough to look at the closure for pow above. If it included the values of all function symbols in scope, it would need an entry for pow itself, which would need an entry for pow, etc.

Whatever way the environment is defined, we need the following operations:

$$\begin{array}{lll} Val & lookup & (Ident\ x, Env\ \gamma) \\ Env & update & (Env\ \gamma, Ident\ x, Val\ v) \end{array}$$

The lookup function has to implement the **overshadowing** of identifiers:

- a variable overshadows a function symbol;

- an inner variable overshadows an outer variable.

These are normal conventions in functional languages and really just consequences of the simple rule that, in $\lambda x \to e$, the *free occurrences* of x get bound in e. For instance, in the expression

```
\x -> \x -> x + x
```

it is the second lambda that binds both variables in x + x. An application

```
(\x -> \x -> x + x) 2 3
```

therefore gives the result $3 + 3 = 6$.

With the environment machinery in place, we can start writing syntax-directed interpreter code based on operational semantics. Integer literals need no further evaluation:

> $eval(\gamma, i)$:
> > **return** i

Alternatively, we can return $i\{\}$, if we uniformly want closures as values.

Variable expressions need lookup. The result is generally a closure, which might need further evaluation. This is certainly the case with call by name, but also happens if the "variable" is a function symbol—for instance, we do not want to evaluate the **main** function before we put it into the symbol table! Therefore:

> $eval(\gamma, x)$:
> > $e\{\delta\} := lookup(\gamma, x)$
> > $eval(\langle functions(\gamma), \delta \rangle, e)$

In the pseudocode, we split the environment into a pair $\langle functions, variables \rangle$, with separate storage for functions and variables. While lookup needs to access them both, the evaluation of the result retains the functions but replaces the variables by the ones found in lookup.

Arithmetic operations are reduced to corresponding integer operations in the implementation language, for instance,

> $eval(\gamma, a + b)$:
> > $u := eval(\gamma, a)$
> > $v := eval(\gamma, b)$
> > **return** $u + v$

The $+$ on the last line is integer addition on the value level. It fails if the values are not integers. But as long as the language has no type checker, we will know this only at run time. Notice, moreover, that this rule can only be applied if u and v are fully evaluated integers. The less than operator $<$ has a similar rule, returning 1 if the comparison is true, 0 if it is false.

If-then-else expressions are interpreted lazily, even if we use call by value as the general strategy:

$$eval(\gamma, \text{if } c \text{ then } a \text{ else } b):$$
$$\quad u := eval(\gamma, c)$$
$$\quad \textbf{if } u = 1$$
$$\quad\quad eval(\gamma, a)$$
$$\quad \textbf{else}$$
$$\quad\quad eval(\gamma, b)$$

Abstractions simply return closures with the variables of the current environment:

$$eval(\gamma, \lambda x.b):$$
$$\quad \textbf{return } (\lambda x.b)\{variables(\gamma)\}$$

Notice that we take only the variables of the environment into the closure, not the function symbols.

Application is the most complex case. Here is a general rule, which works for both call by value and call by name strategies. The decision is made in just one point: when deciding what value to use for the bound variable when evaluating the body.

$$eval(\gamma, (f\ a)):$$
$$\quad (\lambda x.b)\{\delta\} := eval(\gamma, f)$$
$$\quad \textbf{if } call\_by\_value$$
$$\quad\quad u := eval(\gamma, a)$$
$$\quad \textbf{else}$$
$$\quad\quad u := a\{variables(\gamma)\}$$
$$\quad eval(update(\langle functions(\gamma), \delta\rangle, x, u), b)$$

Following these guidelines, a complete interpreter can be implemented with less than 100 lines of Haskell code or a little more Java code. The interpreter can be made parametrized on evaluation strategy, which is passed as a flag when the interpreter is called. This makes it easy to experiment with the strategies. For instance, the example code above (with `main = pow 30`) is reasonably fast with call by value but hopelessly slow with call by name. The example in Section 7.5 (with `main = first 5 infinity`) loops or crashes with call by value but runs fast with call by name.

What about **call by need** (lazy evaluation)? One way to implement it is precisely the same as call by name, except that looking up a variable forces an evaluation of the value of that variable in the environment. The interpreter thus has to be able to change the environment, as was done with the imperative language. In Chapter 5, we did this by explicitly returning a new environment in evaluation. But one could also follow the code generator in Chapter 6, where the environment was a global variable that could be changed.

7.7 Type checking functional languages*

The language we have worked with has a type system known as the **simply typed lambda calculus**. It has two kinds of types:

- basic types, such as `int`;

- function types $A \to B$, where A and B are types.

Simple as the system is, it is much more powerful than the type system we used for the imperative language in Chapter 4. The power comes from the unconstrained generation of function types from any other types, giving rise to functions of functions, and so on. For example,

```
int -> int
(int -> int) -> int
int -> (int -> int)
((int -> int) -> int) -> int
```

In Section 7.2, we gave rules for this type system and explained the method of currying, implying that we only need one-place functions.

A type checker could be implemented in the usual way by converting the typing rules to type checking and inference code. Some care is thereby needed, though. Starting with the abstraction rule,

$$\frac{\Gamma, x : A \vdash b : B}{\Gamma \vdash \lambda x.b : A \to B}$$

it is easy to define type checking:

$$check(\Gamma, \lambda x.b, A \to B) :$$
$$check(extend(\Gamma, x, A), b, B)$$

But what happens if we need type inference? Before even trying to formulate type inference for lambda abstracts, we can simply notice that the expression

```
\x -> x
```

has infinitely many types:

```
int                     -> int
(int -> int)            -> (int -> int)
(int -> int -> int) -> (int -> int -> int)
```

In fact, it has all types of the form

```
A -> A
```

whatever type A is. Hence it is *impossible* to do type inference for all expressions of our functional language, if we expect to return a unique type in simple type theory.

One way to solve the type inference problem for lambda abstracts is to change their syntax, so that it includes type information:

$$\lambda x : t.b$$

But a more common solution is to make the type system **polymorphic**. This means that one and the same expression can have many types.

7.8   Polymorphism*

The polymorphism idea was introduced in ML in the 1970's and inherited by Haskell in the 1990's. It also inspired the **template system** of C++. Taking the simplest possible example, the identity function of last section, we can write

```
// id : A -> A
template<class A> A id(A x)
{
   return x ;
}
```

Two decades later, it was introduced in Java's **generics** (Java 1.5):

```
// id : A -> A
public static <A> A id(A x)
{
   return x ;
}
```

In both cases, polymorphism is expressed by using a **type variable**, A. As a matter of convention, C++ and Java use capital letters as type variables, whereas Haskell uses small letters; in Haskell, capital letters are reserved for constant types.

In C++ and Java, calls to polymorphic functions must indicate the actual types. In ML and Haskell, this is not required. As one of the most remarkable results of programming language theory, type inference works even then! The idea is called **Hindley-Milner polymorphism**. It allows an algorithm which, for any expression of the functional language, returns its **most general type**. Here are some examples of such most general types:

```
(\x -> x)              : a -> a
(\x -> \y -> x)        : a -> b -> a
```

```
(\f -> \x -> f (f x)) : (a -> a) -> a -> a
(\x -> x + x)              : int -> int
```

Notice that different variables mean more generality than the same variable. For example, `a -> b` is more general than `a -> a`, because it doesn't force `a` and `b` to be the same.

Let us take one of the examples into detailed consideration. We start the procedure by introducing a variable `t` for the type:

```
(\f -> \x -> f (f x)) : t
```

Since the expression is a double abstraction, `t` must be a function type:

```
t = a -> b -> c
```

The body of the expression must of course obey this type:

```
f (f x) : c
```

Since `f` is used as a function here, it must have a function type:

```
f : d -> e
```

But since `f` is the variable bound by the first lambda, we also have

```
f : a
```

and hence,

```
a = d -> e
```

Thus the result of applying `f` must have type `e`. But it must also have type `c`, because `f (f x) :   c`. What is more, it must also have type `d`, because `f` can be applied to its own result. Hence

```
c = e = d
```

The type of `x` is on one hand `b` (as the second abstracted variable), on the other hand `d` (because `f` applies to `x`). Hence

```
c = e = b = d
```

and, since `a = d -> e`,

```
a = d -> d
```

We can now conclude with

```
t = (d -> d) -> d -> d
```

as the most general type we managed to find for the expression.

The procedure we followed was completely heuristic—a little bit like solving a Sudoku. Fortunately, there is a mechanical algorithm for the same task. This algorithm is based on **unification**, which is a general method for solving a set of equations between expressions that contain variables.

Exercise 7-0. Infer the most general types of the flip and composition functions,

```
\f -> \x -> \y -> f y x
\g -> \f -> \x -> g (f x)
```

Exercise 7-1. Add a mechanism of templates (generics) to CPP, permitting functions such as the **id** function above, with arbitrary many type arguments. Write the new grammar rules that are needed, as well as the typing rules for function definitions and calls. You can use either C++ or Java syntax.

7.9   Polymorphic type checking with unification*

Polymorphic type inference finds the most general type possible for a given expression. The inference function works in the usual way of syntax-directed translation, performing pattern matching on the expression. What it returns is not just the type of the expression, but also a **substitution**, which maps type variables to types (which can themselves contain variables). Just like the type checker of Chapter 4, we also need a **context** that stores the types of the variables in the expression. Notice the difference between these mappings: both of them store types as values, but the context gives the types of the variables in the source code expression, whereas the substitution gives the values of the type variables created by the type checker itself.

In the type inference pseudocode, we will define the function

$\langle Subst, Type \rangle$ *infer(Exp e)*

We thus keep the context implicit, like in the code generator of Section 6.3. But we can access the environment with *lookup*, *extend*, and *free* functions; *free* means undoing the effect of *extend*:

Type lookup (Ident x)

Void extend (Ident x, Type t)

Void free (Ident x)

The implicit environment also takes care of generating fresh type variables,

    Ident fresh ()

A substitution γ can be applied to a type t, which means replacing the type variables in t with their values as given in γ. (Substitution in types is simpler than substitution in expressions, because there are no variable bindings in types. This is one reason why we avoided substitutions in the interpreter and used closures instead.) We write

$$t\gamma$$

to apply the substitution γ to the type t. As an example of a substitution and its application,

```
(a -> c -> d){a:= d -> d, c:=d, b:=d} ⇓ (d -> d) -> d -> d
```

is one that could have been used at a certain point in the type inference of the previous section.

    Now we are ready to start defining type inference. Constants and variables are simple, and return the empty substitution {}:

    infer(i) :
       return $\langle \{\}, Int \rangle$

    infer(x) :
       $t := lookup(x)$
       return $\langle \{\}, t \rangle$

For lambda abstracts, we introduce a fresh type variable for the bound variable; this represents the argument type of the function. Then we infer the type of the body. This inference returns a substitution, which we have to apply to the argument type variable, since it may give it a value. After the inference of the body, we must discard the latest variable x from the context:

    infer($\lambda x.b$) :
       $a := fresh()$
       $extend(x, a)$
       $\langle \gamma, t \rangle := infer(b)$
       $free(x)$
       return $\langle \gamma, a\gamma \rightarrow t \rangle$

    As a first example, let us infer the type of the identity function by following the rules. We write this in the same format as the definition of the *infer* function, showing the actual values returned at each stage. We also make the context explicit when relevant:

$infer(\lambda x.x)$:
   $a := fresh()$
   $extend(x, a)$
   $\langle \{\}, a \rangle := infer(x)$ // in context $x : a$
   return $\langle \{\}, a\{\} \rightarrow a \rangle$

By applying the empty substitution, we get the final type $a \rightarrow a$.

The most complicated case of type inference is function application:

$infer(f\ a)$:
   $\langle \gamma_1, t_1 \rangle := infer(f)$
   $\langle \gamma_2, t_2 \rangle := infer(a)$
   $v := fresh()$
   $\gamma_3 := mgu(t_1\gamma_2,\ t_2 \rightarrow v)$
   return $\langle \gamma_3 \circ \gamma_2 \circ \gamma_1,\ v\gamma_3 \rangle$

The types of the function and the argument are inferred first. To combine all information obtained, the type of the function is refined by applying the substitution received from the argument, obtaining $t_1\gamma_2$. The type is then expressed in terms of the inferred argument type t_2 and an unknown value type, which is represented by a fresh type variable v. These two types are sent to **unification**, mgu. This gives yet another substitution γ_3, which is applied to the value type. All information is finally gathered in the **composition of substitutions** $\gamma_3 \circ \gamma_2 \circ \gamma_1$, which is returned together with the value type. The composition of substitutions is defined via their application, in a way similar to the usual composition of functions:

$$t(\delta \circ \gamma) = (t\gamma)\delta$$

It remains to define unification, mgu. It takes two types and returns their **most general unifier**, which is a substitution γ that gives the same result when applied to any of the two types. In other words,

$$t(mgu(t, u)) = u(mgu(t, u))$$

Of course, mgu can also fail, if the types are not unifiable.

$Subst\ mgu\ (Type\ t,\ Type\ u)$

$mgu(a_1 \rightarrow b_1,\ a_2 \rightarrow b_2)$: // both are function types
   $\gamma_1 := mgu(a_1,\ a_2)$
   $\gamma_2 := mgu(b_1\gamma_1,\ b_2\gamma_1)$
   return $\gamma_2 \circ \gamma_1$

$mgu(v, t)$: // the first type is a type variable
   if $t = v$

          return {}
       else if $occurs(v, t)$
          fail (''occurs check'')
       else
          return $\{v := t\}$

$mgu(t, v)$: // the second type is a type variable
    $mgu(v, t)$

$mgu(t, u)$: // other cases: succeeds only for equal types
    if $t = u$
       return {}
    else
       fail (''types not unifiable'')

There are thus two reasons why types may not unify. They can just be different types, as in the last case. It rejects for instance the unification of `Int` with `Double`, and `Int` with a function type. Or the unification can fail in the so-called **occurs check**: if the type variable v occurs in the type t, the types are not unifiable. This check rejects, for instance, the unification of v with $v \to u$. If the occurs check were not performed, the algorithm would return the substitution

$$\{v := v \to u\}$$

which would only be satisfied by an "infinite type" of the form $(\ldots (v \to u) \ldots \to u) \to u$

    To see the type inference for function applications at work, together with occurs check, let us trace one more example:

   $infer(\lambda x.(x\ x))$:
     $a := fresh()$
     $\langle \gamma, t \rangle := infer(x\ x)$: // in context $x : a$
       $\langle \{\}, a \rangle := infer(x)$
       $\langle \{\}, a \rangle := infer(x)$
       $b := fresh()$
       $\gamma := mgu(a, a \to b)$:
         fail (''occurs check'')

On the last line, *mgu* fails because of occurs check: a cannot unify with $a \to b$. In other words, a function cannot be applied to itself.

Exercise 7-2. Trace the type inference algorithm and unification with the expression `\f -> \x -> f (f x)`.

Exercise 7-3. Extend type inference and unification to pair and list types. Can you find a generalization that makes this possible without adding new cases to the function definitions?

Exercise 7-4.+ Implement the unification algorithm and type inference for expressions. Try them out with all the examples discussed.

Exercise 7-5. Even if (\x -> (x x)) fails to type check, a "self-application" is completely legal in (\x -> x)(\x -> x). Can you explain why?

Chapter 8

The Language Design Space

The functional language shown in the previous chapter was very simple, but it can be made even simpler: the minimal language of lambda calculus has just three grammar rules. It needs no integers, no booleans—almost nothing, since everything can be defined by those three rules. This leads us to the notion of Turing Completeness, which defines what a general-purpose programming language must be able to do. In addition to lambda calculus, we will show another Turing complete language, which is an imperative language similar to C, but still definable on less than ten lines. Looking at these languages gives us tools to assess the popular thesis that "it doesn't matter what language you use, since it's the same old Turing machine anyway".

If you work as a programmer, you are not likely to implement a general-purpose programming language in your professional career. You are much more likely to implement a **DSL, domain-specific language**. However, the things you have learned by going through the assignments give you all the tools you need to create your own language. You will feel confident to do this, and you also know the limits of what is realistic and what is not. The design space reaches from the simplest possible languages to ones that look like natural language. Such languages can be useful in, for instance, speech-based interfaces. But they also give you an idea of what is reasonable to expect from natural language processing and how it relates to compiler construction.

This chapter provides the concepts and tools needed for solving Assignment 6 in a satisfactory way—creating a domain-specific query language. But it is your own imagination and willingness to learn more that set the limits of what you can achieve.

8.1   How simple can a language be?

In the 1930's, before electronic computers were built, mathematicians developed **models of computation** trying to define what it means to be computable in principle. The background of this was in the foundation of mathematics, where the question was whether all mathematical problems can be solved mechanically. To answer this question, one had to define what it means to solve a problem mechanically—in principle, rather than in practice.

The research resulted in several models, of which the most well-known are

- **Turing Machine** (Alan Turing), similar to imperative programming.

- **Lambda Calculus** (Alonzo Church), similar to functional programming.

- **Recursive Functions** (Stephen Kleene), also similar to functional programming.

It was soon proved that these models are equivalent: although they express programs and computation in very different ways, they cover exactly the same programs. And the solvability of mathematical problems got a negative answer: it is not possible to construct a machine that can solve all problems. One of the counter-examples is the **halting problem**: it was proved by Turing that there cannot be any program (i.e. any Turing machine) which decides for any given program and input if the program terminates with that input.

The models of computation also became prototypes for programming languages, corresponding to the different **programming language paradigms** still in use today. Thus the Turing Machine itself was the prototypical imperative language. Lambda Calculus was the prototypical functional language, but the way programs are usually written looks more like recursive functions. The term **Turing-completeness** is used for any programming language that is equivalent to any of these models, that is, equivalent to the Turing Machine.

All general-purpose programming languages used today are Turing-complete. But this doesn't say very much: actually, a language can be *very* simple and still Turing-complete.

8.2   Pure lambda calculus as a programming language*

As the simplest model syntactically, let us look at lambda calculus. The minimal definition of the language needs just three constructs: variables, applications, and abstractions:

```
Exp ::= Ident | Exp Exp | "\" Ident "->" Exp
```

This language is called the **pure lambda calculus**. It doesn't even need integer constants, because they can be defined as follows:

```
0 = \f -> \x -> x
1 = \f -> \x -> f x
2 = \f -> \x -> f (f x)
3 = \f -> \x -> f (f (f x))
...
```

In other words: number n is a higher-order function that applies any function f, to any argument x, n times.

The functions 0,1,2,... are known as **Church numerals**. Now we must show that they can really be used as integers. In other words, we must show that we can do normal arithmetic with them. We start by defining addition:

```
PLUS = \m -> \n -> \f -> \x -> n f (m f x)
```

The intuition is: when you add n to m, you get a function that applies f first m times and then n times. Altogether, you apply f to x $m + n$ times.

Here is an example. You may want to carry it out in more detail by using the operational semantics of the previous chapter.

```
PLUS 2 3
= (\m -> \n -> \f -> \x -> n f (m f x))
     (\f -> \x -> f (f x)) (\f -> \x -> f (f (f x)))
= \f -> \x -> (\f -> \x -> f (f (f x)))
     f ((\f -> \x -> f (f x)) f x)
= \f -> \x -> (\f -> \x -> f (f (f x))) f (f (f x))
= \f -> \x -> f (f (f (f (f x))))
= 5
```

Now it is easy to define multiplication:

```
MULT = \m -> \n -> m (PLUS n) 0
```

The idea is to add n to 0 m times.

In addition to integers to represent data, a programming language needs **control structures** to organize computations. In the functional language of the previous section, we had a primitive if-then-else structure. But such structures can actually be defined in pure lambda calculus. The first step is to use a proper representation of booleans—not as integers 0 and 1, but as the so-called **Church booleans**, which are the following functions:

```
TRUE  = \x -> \y -> x
FALSE = \x -> \y -> y
```

The idea is that a boolean performs a choice from two arguments. TRUE chooses the first, FALSE the second. (Thus FALSE happens to be equal to 0 after all, by renaming of bound variables.) This property is put to use in the conditional expression, which expects a Church boolean as its first argument, and the "if" and "else" values as additional arguments:

```
IFTHENELSE = \b -> \x -> \y -> b x y
```

The boolean connectives can be defined in terms of conditionals:

```
AND = \a -> \b -> IFTHENELSE a b FALSE
OR  = \a -> \b -> IFTHENELSE a TRUE b
```

As a slight difference from the standard treatment, conditionals and connectives in pure lambda calculus are not necessarily lazy. Their laziness depends on evaluation strategy: if call by value is used, they cannot be lazy, but with call by name they are. In other words, using pure lambda calculus as programming language makes it hard to maintain exceptions to the general evaluation strategy.

To be fully expressive, functional programs must also be able to do **recursion**. In the language of the last chapter, this was easy because the language had a mechanism for defining functions, and the defined function could appear on the right hand side: for instance,

```
 fact n = if x == 0 then 1 else n * fact (n - 1)
```

defines the factorial ($n!$). In pure lambda calculus, however, such definitions are not available. The "definitions" we have shown above are not part of the language, but just something that we use for introducing shorthands for long expressions. A shorthand must always be possible to eliminate from an expression. Using the defined name on the right hand side would create a circular definition, and the name would be impossible to eliminate.

Thus the most amazing invention in pure lambda calculus is perhaps the possibility to express recursion. This can be done with the **fix-point combinator**, also known as the **Y combinator**, which is the function

```
Y = \g -> (\x -> g (x x)) (\x -> g (x x))
```

This function has the property

```
Y g = g (Y g)
```

which means that Y iterates g infinitely many times. You can easily verify this property by taking a couple of computation steps (exercise).

The factorial can be defined in terms of the fix-point combinator as follows:

```
FACT =
  Y (\f -> \n -> IFTHENELSE (ISZERO n) 1 (MULT n (f (PRED n))))
```

This corresponds very closely to the intuitive recursive definition, using the Church numerals, booleans, and conditionals. It needs two auxiliary concepts: `ISZERO` to decide if a numeral is equal to 0, and `PRED` to find the previous numeral (i.e. $n - 1$, except 0 for 0). These are defined as follows:

```
ISZERO = \n -> n (\x -> FALSE) TRUE
PRED =
  \n -> \f -> \x -> n (\g -> \h -> h (g f)) (\u -> x) (\u -> u)
```

The definition of `PRED` is rather complex; you might want to try and verify at least that `PRED 1` is 0.

To write programs in pure lambda calculus is certainly possible! But it is inconvenient and inefficient. However, it is a good starting point for a language to have a very small **core language**. The implementation (compiler, interpreter) is then built for the core language with syntactic sugar and possibly optimizations. For instance, the functional language of Chapter 7 has built-in integers as an optimization. Among real-world languages, Lisp is built from lambda calculus with very few additions, such as a primitive notion of lists. Haskell has a small core language based on lambda calculus with algebraic datatypes and pattern matching, as well as primitive number types.

Exercise 8-0. Show the Y combinator property

```
Y g = g (Y g)
```

Exercise 8-1. Show that `PRED 1 = 0` with Church numerals.

Exercise 8-2. Define the exponentiation of Church numerals, that is, a function `EXP` such that `EXP m n` corresponds to m^n and multiplies m with itself n times.

Exercise 8-3. Try to infer the types of the Church numerals 0 and 1, `PLUS`, `IFTHENELSE`, and the Y combinator. If you don't manage by hand, use the algorithm of Section 7.9—or just the type inference command `:t` of the Haskell interpreter `ghci`.

8.3 Another Turing-complete language*

BF, Brainfuck, is a language designed by Urban Müller as a variant of the theoretical language **P"** by Corrado Böhm. The goal was to create a Turing-complete language with the smallest possible compiler. Müller's compiler was 240 bytes in size.

A BF program has one implicit byte pointer, called "the pointer", which is free to move around within an array of bytes, initially all set to zero. The pointer itself is initialized to point to the beginning of this array. The language has eight commands, each of which is expressed by a single character:

>	increment the pointer
<	decrement the pointer
+	increment the byte at the pointer
−	decrement the byte at the pointer
.	output the byte at the pointer
,	input a byte and store it in the byte at the pointer
[	jump forward past the matching] if the byte at the pointer is 0
]	jump backward to the matching [unless the byte at the pointer is 0

All other characters are treated as comments and thereby ignored.

Here is an example of a BF program: `char.bf`, displaying the ASCII character set (from 0 to 255):

```
.+[.+]
```

Here is the program `hello.bf`, which prints "Hello"

```
++++++++++            Set counter 10 for iteration
[>+++++++>++++++++++<<-] Set up 7 and 10 on array and iterate
>++.                  Print 'H'
>+.                   Print 'e'
+++++++.              Print 'l'
.                     Print 'l'
+++.                  Print 'o'
```

Exercise 8-4. Define integer addition in BF. You can first restrict it to numbers whose size is one byte, then try to be more ambitious.

Exercise 8-5. Write an interpreter of BF and try it out on `char.bf` and `hello.bf`.

Exercise 8-6. Write a compiler of BF via translation to C:

>	`++p;`
<	`--p;`
+	`++*p;`
−	`--*p;`
.	`putchar(*p);`
,	`*p = getchar();`
[	`while (*p) {`
]	`}`

The code should appear within a `main ()` function, which initializes the storage and the pointer as follows:

```
char a[30000];
char *p = a;
```

Test your compiler with the BF programs presented in this section. The array size 30,000 comes from the original BF definition; to make BF truly Turing-complete you can think of it as infinite.

8.4   Criteria for a good programming language

Pure lambda calculus, BF, and the fragment of C corresponding to BF suggest that Turing completeness might not be enough for a good programming language. There are many other reasonable criteria:

- **Orthogonality**: the set of language constructs should be small and non-overlapping.

- **Succinctness**: the language should permit short expressions of ideas.

- **Efficiency**: the language should permit writing code that runs fast and in small space.

- **Clarity**: the language should permit writing programs that are easy to understand.

- **Safety**: the language should guard against fatal errors.

These criteria are obviously not always compatible, but there are trade-offs. For instance, pure lambda calculus and BF obviously satisfy orthogonality, but hardly any of the other criteria. Haskell and C++ are known for providing many ways to do the same things, and therefore blamed for lack of orthogonality. But they are certainly good at many other counts.

In practice, different languages are good for different applications. For instance, BF can be good for reasoning about computability. There may also be languages that aren't good for any applications. And even good languages can be implemented in bad ways, let alone used in bad ways.

We suggested in Chapter 1 that languages are evolving toward higher and higher levels, as a result of improved compiler technology and more powerful computers. This creates more work for machines (and for compiler writers!) but relieves the burden of language users. Here are some trends that can be observed in the history:

- Toward more **structured programming** (from GOTOs to `while` loops to recursion).

- Toward richer **type systems** (from bit strings to numeric types to structures to algebraic data types to dependent types).

- Toward more **abstraction** (from character arrays to strings, from arrays to vectors and lists, from unlimited access to abstract data types).

- Toward more **generality** (from cut-and-paste to macros to functions to polymorphic functions to first-class modules).

- Toward more **streamlined syntax** (from positions and line numbers, keywords used as identifiers, `begin` and `end` markers, limited-size identifiers, etc, to a "C-like" syntax that can be processed with standard tools and defined in pure BNF).

8.5   Domain-specific languages

As different languages are good for different purposes, why not turn the perspective and create the best language for each purpose? Such languages are called **special-purpose languages**, **minilanguages**, or **domain-specific languages, DSL**'s.

Here are some examples of DSL's:

- Lex for lexers, Yacc for parsers;

- BNFC for compiler front ends;

- XML for structuring documents;

- `make` for specifying compilation commands;

- `bash` (a Unix shell) for working on files and directories;

- PostScript for printing documents;

- JavaScript for dynamic web pages.

DSL's have their own design decisions:

- Imperative or declarative?

- Interpreted or compiled?

- Portable or platform-dependent?

- Statically or dynamically checked?

- Turing-complete or limited?

- Language or library?

Making a DSL Turing-complete means that it has, in theory at least, the same power as general-purpose languages. PostScript and JavaScript are examples of DSL's that actually are Turing-complete. But the extra power comes with the price that their halting problem is undecidable. Consequently, there are no complexity guarantees for programs. For instance, a parser written in a general-purpose language can be exponential or even loop infinitely, whereas a parser written in BNFC is guaranteed to run in linear time.

Nevertheless, there is a rationale for DSL's which are not languages at all, but just libraries in general-purpose programming languages. They are known as **embedded languages**.

8.6 Embedded languages*

An embedded language is a minilanguage that is a fragment of a larger **host language**. Implementing a DSL as an embedded language has several advantages:

- It inherits the implementation of the host language.

- No extra training is needed for those who already know the host language.

- There is an unlimited access to "language extensions" via using the host language.

There are also disadvantages:

- One cannot reason about the embedded language independently of the host language.

- Unlimited access to host language can compromise safety, efficiency, etc.

- An embedded language may be difficult to interface with other languages than the host language.

- Training programmers previously unfamiliar with the host language can have a large overhead.

A standard example of embedded languages are the **parser combinators** of Haskell. They are often used as an alternative to grammar formalisms. Thus they enable the writing of recursive-descent parsers directly in Haskell, but in a clearer and more succinct way than raw coding without the combinators (cf. Section 3.6).

At this point, you might want to skip the rest of this section if you are not a Haskell-programmer, since we will show some unfamiliar notation without further explanation. In Figure 8.1, we define a complete parser combinator library for context-free grammars (and beyond). The library has functions for the basic operations of sequencing (. . .), union (∥∥), and literals (`lit`). These operators are familiar from regular expressions (Section 3.2). But they have the power to deal with arbitrary context-free grammars, and even beyond, because they allow recursive definitions of parsing functions in the style of LL(k) parsing (Section 3.6).

An example of the use of the combinators is the definition of the if/while language of Section 3.6, with the BNF grammar

```
SIf.    Stm ::= "if" "(" Exp ")" Stm ;
SWhile. Stm ::= "while" "(" Exp ")" Stm ;
SExp.   Stm ::= Exp ;
EInt.   Exp ::= Integer ;
```

If we work with the combinators, we must first define the abstract syntax datatypes manually:

```
data Stm = SIf Exp Stm | SWhile Exp Stm | SExp Exp
data Exp = EInt Integer
```

Then we define the parser functions, using objects of types `Stm` and `Exp` as values. The terminals of the BNF grammar are treated by the `lit` function, and the nonterminals by calls to the parsing functions. Semantic actions are used for building the abstract syntax trees.

```
pStm :: Parser String Stm
pStm = lit "if" ... lit "(" ... pExp ... lit ")" ... pStm ***
        (\ (_,(_,(e,(_,s)))) -> SIf e s)
    |||
       lit "while" ... lit "(" ... pExp ... lit ")" ... pStm ***
        (\ (_,(_,(e,(_,s)))) -> SWhile e s)
    |||
       pExp ... lit ";" *** (\ (e,_) -> SExp e)

pExp :: Parser String Exp
pExp = satisfy (all isDigit) *** (\i -> EInt (read i))
```

```
infixr 4 ...
infixl 3 ***
infixl 2 |||

-- read input [a], return value b and the rest of the input
type Parser a b - [a] -> [(b,[a])]

-- sequence: combine two parser
(...) :: Parser a b -> Parser a c -> Parser a (b,c)
(p ... q) s = [((x,y),r) | (x,t) <- p s, (y,r) <- q t]

-- union: two alternative parsers
(|||) :: Parser a b -> Parser a b -> Parser a b
(p ||| q) s = p s ++ q s

-- recognize a token that satisfies a predicate
satisfy :: (a -> Bool) -> Parser a a
satisfy b (c:cs) = [(c,cs) | b c]
satisfy _ _ = []

-- literal: recognize a given string (special case of satisfy)
lit :: (Eq a) => a -> Parser a a
lit a = satisfy (==a)

-- semantic action: apply a function to parse results
(***) :: Parser a b -> (b -> c) -> Parser a c
(p *** f) s = [(f x,r) | (x,r) <- p s]
```

Figure 8.1: A parser combinator library in Haskell.

The example shows that combinators require more code to be written manually than in BNFC, where the grammar is enough. On the other hand, the run-time code becomes smaller, because no bulky Happy-generated files are needed.

Moreover, combinators have more expressive power than BNFC. In particular, they can deal with **ambiguity**, because the `Parser` type is a list of all parse results, not only one. They are not even limited to context-free languages; writing a parser for the copy language is left as an exercise. This extra power is in practice often the main reason to use combinators rather than BNF grammars.

As recursive descent parsers in general, the combinators loop with left-recursive rules. Left recursion must thus be manually eliminated, as shown in Section 3.6. LL(1) conflicts as such are not a problem. But without left factoring, parsers that have to inspect many paths can become very slow, because they have to do **backtracking** from unsuccessful paths. If such things happen, it can be very difficult to find the reason, because there are no automatic diagnostic tools similar to the LALR(1) table construction of Happy.

Our conclusion of parser combinators is that they very closely reflect the pros and cons of embedded languages listed at the beginning of this section. Moreover, BNF grammars are an already established, well-understood language, which has available implementations (e.g. in Happy and, as a front-end to it, in BNFC). Therefore there is little reason to use parser combinators except when the additional power is needed or as a test case for functional programming techniques, which in fact is a very common use.

All this said, there are plenty of cases where an embedded language can be the best choice. For instance, it would be overkill to define a separate language for arithmetic expressions, because they are so well supported in standard programming languages. There are many cases where a well-defined library works almost like a language of its own—for instance, in C++, where the **Standard Template Library** gives a high-level access to data structures freeing application programmers from details such as memory management.

Also the problem of complexity guarantees, which we encountered in the case of parser combinators, can be overcome by using types as a control mechanism. We could for instance have a similar set of combinators as in Figure 8.1, but with finite automata as target type:

```
(...) :: Aut a -> Aut a -> Aut a
(p ... q) s = sequenceAut p q

(|||) :: Aut a -> Aut a -> Aut a
(p ||| q) s = unionAut p q

lit :: a -> Aut a
lit s = symbolAut s
```

The value of a combinator application is then always an automaton, which are built by the NFA operations described in Section 3.3. The automaton can be further processed by determination and minimization. A language defined in this way will always be recognizable by a finite automaton in linear time, as guaranteed by the type `Aut`.

Exercise 8-7. Add a rule for `if` statements with `else` to the example language. Construct a statement with the dangling else behaviour (Section 3.8), and test how the combinator parser deals with it.

Exercise 8-8. Write a combinator parser for the copy language (Section 3.9).

8.7 Case study: BNFC as a domain-specific language

The first version of BNFC was released in 2002. It targeted Haskell with Happy and Alex. In 2003, it was ported to Java, C, and C++; in 2005, to Java 1.5; and in 2006, to OCaml and C#. In 2006, BNFC became a part of the "stable" Debian Linux distriburion. Since then, it has changed only minimally, mostly to preserve compatibility with the targeted tools, whenever these tools have had backward-incompatible changes.

The goal of BNFC is to implement exactly the idea that a parser returns an abstract syntax tree built from the trees for the nonterminal items by using the rule label. If the parser is limited in this way, more general tools such as Yacc and Happy, let alone parser combinators in a general-purpose language, are unnecessarily powerful. Thus limiting the expressive power and specializing the purpose of the language, BNFC helps programmers to achieve the following goals:

- to save writing code,

- to keep the different compiler modules in sync,

- to use the grammar as reliable documentation,

- to guarantee the symmetry of parser and pretty printer (useful in e.g. source code optimizations),

- to be sure of the complexity of parsing,

- to be able to port the same grammar to different host languages.

In practice, the first goal is often the most important one. Not only are programmers lazy, but they also know that short programs are more reliable. Eric S. Raymond, in *The Art of Unix Programming*, refers to surveys according to which

> *The number of bugs per line is independent of programming language.*

As a concrete evidence for the brevity of BNFC, compare the size of BNFC source code of the language implemented in Section 2.10 (CPP.cf) with the size of generated code in some target languages. For comparison, we also take the raw C++ code, that is, the code generated by Bison and Flex. The figures show that Bison and Flex just about halve the total size of the code needed to be written, whereas BNFC shrinks it by almost two orders of magnitude!

format	CPP.cf	Haskell	Java 1.5	C++	raw C++
files	1	9	55	12	12
lines	63	999	3353	5382	9424
chars	1548	28516	92947	96587	203659
chars target/src	1	18	60	62	132

Of course, C++ and other programmers can write shorter code than this by hand, and they might not need all of the components generated by BNFC (for instance, the documentation). Moreover, BNFC might not be powerful enough, for instance, if the language to be implemented is not context-free. But even for such projects, it can be a good starting point to write an approximative BNF grammar and let BNFC produce the boilerplate code that serves as a starting point.

In Section 8.4, we summarized a set of language design questions. Let us look at the decisions made in the case of BNFC:

- *Imperative or declarative?* Declarative. BNFC just defines the grammar, and uses separate algorithms that work on all grammars.

- *Interpreted or compiled?* Compiled. BNFC code is translated to host language code.

- *Portable or platform-dependent?* Portable. BNFC is designed to work with many host languages.

- *Statically checked?* Yes, some consistency checks are made before generating the host language code. But more checks would be desirable, for instance, the check for LALR conflicts.

- *Turing-complete or limited?* Limited. The grammars are limited to a subset of context-free grammars.

- *Language or library?* Language, with its own syntax, semantics, and compiler. And the need of some learning.

The most important lesson from BNFC is perhaps that its declarativity makes it both succinct, portable, and predictable. Using Happy, CUP, or Bison directly would be none of these, because any host language code can be inserted in the semantic actions.

The things that are not so good in BNFC involve more the implementation than the language itself:

Static checking should be closer to BNFC source. We already mentioned the checking of conflicts. Another known issue is the use of identifiers. Using the same identifier both as category and constructor is legal in Haskell but not in Java. This gives errors, about which only a warning is issued. But if the warning is ignored, hard to understand Java errors may arise.

The *maintenance* of the BNFC code base is made difficult by the multitude of different host languages. The standard lexer and parser tools are not always backward-compatible, and since updating BNFC lags behind, users may need to use older versions of these tools. Maintenance is further complicated by the fact that the source code of BNFC has become a mess and is hard to understand.

8.8 Using BNFC for implementing languages

The main advantage of BNFC is perhaps that it makes it easy to get started with a new language. A prototype with a dozen rules can be ready to run in five minutes.

Usually, it is good to start with a set of code examples. If you are implementing an already existing language, as in Assignments 1 to 5 of this book, such examples typically exist in abundance. But if you are designing your own language, a good way to start is to write some code in this language as if it already existed. When writing the code and seeing the code you just wrote, you will get ideas for how to make the language really nice—into a language of your dreams. You should write both small examples, focusing on individual features, and large examples, showing how real job is done with your language. You can then start writing your grammar with the goal of parsing your own examples, starting from the simplest ones—in the same way as in Assignment 1.

As your language grows, you should always start by writing examples that cover the new features. Your set of examples will then be a means for **regression testing** of your grammar. Later, they will also guide you with the other components of your compiler or interpreter. The examples will also be an essential part of the documentation of your language, making it easy for others to start coding in it by first modifying your examples. For this purpose, it is important that your examples are meaningful programs that make something useful with the tasks for which your language is designed.

Just like in Assignment 1, you should compile your grammar often and re-run it on the example set. In this process, it may happen that you have to change your design. For instance, it may turn out that some constructs of your language were actually ambiguous; maybe you didn't see this at a first sight, but it was conflicts found in LALR(1) table construction that revealed this. If you find real ambiguities in this way, it is advisable to eliminate them by changing the grammar.

One more advantage with BNFC is that you can change your implementation language. There have been projects where a first prototype implementation was built in Haskell and a later production version in C. The BNF grammar remained unchanged, as the programmers only needed to run `bnfc` with the `-c` option to create the new parser and abstract syntax.

It is also possible to combine implementation languages, because they can communicate via the parser and the pretty printer. Thus one can parse the code in Haskell, make type checking in Haskell, pretty-print the type-annotated trees, and parse the resulting code in a C program that performs the rest of the compilation. This property also makes BNFC usable for defining **data formats**: you can define a structured data representation that permits exchange of data between programs written in different languages. Sometimes such a representation is a good alternative to more standard formats such as **XML**, which is verbose and difficult for humans to read.

In code generation, it may make sense to create a BNFC grammar for the target language as well—even for such a simple language as JVM assembler. This has two advantages:

- code generation produces abstract syntax trees and can ignore some details of the target code concrete syntax;

- target code trees can be processed further, for instance, by optimizations.

Using BNFC also has a price: it forces you to restrict your language to what we like to boldly call **well-behaved languages**. These are the main three restrictions:

- lexing must be strictly finite state;

- parsing must be strictly LALR(1);

- white space cannot be given any meaning, but it is just ignored in lexing (except in string literals).

Surprisingly many legacy languages have constructs that are not "well-behaved". For instance, Haskell violates all the three restrictions. Java and C are largely well-behaved, and have actually BNFC grammars available at BNFC web page. Full C++ requires a much more powerful parser than LR(k) for any k. But often the features that go beyond the "well-behaved" languages can be avoided without any penalty for usability.

In Haskell, **layout syntax** is a feature that violates all of the three requirements. Section A.8 in Appendix A explains how a restricted form of layout syntax can be implemented in BNFC by using preprocessing. Opinions are split about the utility of layout syntax: many programmers think it is a nuisance in Haskell. At the same time, layout syntax has gained new popularity in Python.

One peculiarity of layout syntax is that it breaks the fundamental property of **alpha convertibility**, which says that changing a variable name (in all occurrences) doesn't change the program behaviour. A counterexample in Haskell is

```
eval e = case e of EAdd x y  > eval x + eval y
                   EMul x y -> eval x * eval y
```

If you rename e to `exp`, the code gets a syntax error, because the branch `EAdd` no longer starts from the same column as `EMul`.

8.9 Compiling natural language*

Natural language could be seen as the ultimate limit of bringing a language close to humans. When the first electronic computers were built in the late 1940's, there was a lot of optimism about processing natural language. It was encouraged by the success of cryptography during the Second World War. The idea arose that Russian was like encrypted English, and that it could be cracked with similar methods as Turing and his colleagues had cracked the Germans' Enigma. Now, more than 60 years later and with billions of times more computing power, breaking the Russian "code" (or any other natural language) is still not possible: it is considered one of the hardest problems of computer science, as hard as Artificial Intelligence in general.

Of course, some of the problems encountered 60 years ago have now been overcome, and systems like Google translate work for more than 50 languages. The need for automatic translation is constantly growing, as the internet reaches a majority of the seven billion people on the globe, who speak over 6000 different languages. It is impossible to translate even a small part of the information on the internet into even a small fraction of these languages manually, how ever desirable this might be.

For instance, the Wikipedia encyclopedia is available in around 300 languages. A majority of articles are only available in English, and the occasional manually produced translations often differ in content and coverage. Google translate is not a solution, because its quality is not sufficient. One could say that Google translations are of **browsing quality**: they give an idea of what the documents say. But they do not reach **publishing quality**, which would require an accurate and flawless rendering of the original.

Another important task of natural language processing is **human-computer interaction (HCI)**, where attempts are made to replace the use of computer languages by human language. This language is often very restricted, for instance, voice commands in a car enabling the use of the music player and the navigation system. Unlike machine translation, such systems only have to deal with small parts of language. But they have to do it with precision. The natural choice of techniques is hence similar to compilation: formal grammars and semantic analysis.

8.10   Case study: a query language*

Let us conclude this chapter and this book with an example of using a fragment of natural language as a domain-specific language. The application is a **query language**, which allows its user to ask questions in English. Every question is parsed and sent to a question-answering program, which generates an answer. Here are two example queries and answers:

> *Is any even number prime?*
> Yes.

> *Which numbers greater than 100 and smaller than 150 are prime?*
> 101, 103, 107, 109, 113, 127, 131, 137, 139, 149.

The example system we will build is from mathematics. This is because the question-answering program is then easy to implement by using the computer's standard arithmetic, and we can show a complete system in a small space. But the system is built in such a way that the subject matter would be easy to change, for instance, to cover database queries about films. But even the mathematics system can be interesting, as shown by the popularity of Wolfram Alpha, "the computational knowledge engine".

Here is a BNF grammar for a simple query language:

```
-- general part

    QWhich.     Query     ::= "which" Kind "is" Property ;
    QWhether.   Query     ::= "is" Term Property ;
    TAll.       Term      ::= "every" Kind ;
    TAny.       Term      ::= "any" Kind ;
    PAnd.       Property ::= Property "and" Property ;
    POr.        Property ::= Property "or"  Property ;
    PNot.       Property ::= "not" Property ;
    KProperty.  Kind      ::= Property Kind ;
```

```
-- specific part

  KNumber.    Kind       ::= "number" ;
  TInteger.   Element    ::= Integer ;
  PEven.      Property   ::= "even" ;
  POdd.       Property   ::= "odd" ;
  PPrime.     Property   ::= "prime" ;
  PDivisible. Property   ::= "divisible" "by" Term ;
  PSmaller.   Property   ::= "smaller" "than" Term ;
  PGreater.   Property   ::= "greater" "than" Term ;
```

This grammar is not yet quite what we want; for instance, it says *which number is prime* even though we expect many numbers as an answer and hence *which numbers are prime* would be more adequate. There is also a plain error, that of placing all properties before kinds. This is right for *even number*, but wrong for *greater than 3 number*, which should be *number greater than 3*. Of course, we could solve both issues by more categories and rules, but this would clutter the abstract syntax with semantically irrelevant distinctions, such as singular and plural kinds and pre- and postfix properties.

8.11 Grammatical Framework, GF*

To get the expressive power needed for making the query language really nice, we use **GF**, **Grammatical Framework**. GF is inspired by compiler construction but designed for natural language grammars. It has been applied to dozens of languages ranging from European languages like English and Dutch to Nepali, Swahili, and Thai. GF is moreover able to define translators by using just grammars. You can obtain GF from `grammaticalframework.org`.

The following is a very simple example of a GF grammar:

```
abstract Arithm = {
  cat Exp ;
  fun EInt : Int -> Exp ;
  fun EMul : Exp -> Exp -> Exp ;
  }
concrete ArithmJava of Arithm = {
  lincat Exp = Str ;
  lin EInt i = i.s ;
  lin EMul x y = x ++ "*" ++ y ;
  }
concrete ArithmJVM of Arithm = {
  lincat Exp = Str ;
```

```
lin EInt i = "bipush" ++ i.s ;
lin EMul x y = x ++ y ++ "imul" ;
}
```

This grammar has three GF modules: one **abstract syntax** module `Arithm`, and two **concrete syntax** modules, `ArithmJava` and `ArithmJVM`. If you save the modules in the files `Arithm.gf`, `ArithmJava.gf` and `ArithmJVM.gf`, you can translate Java expressions to JVM expressions, and also vice versa. You first start the `gf` interpreter by the shell command

```
gf ArithmJava.gf ArithmJVM.gf
```

In the shell that opens, you use a pipe to parse from Java and linearize to JVM:

```
> parse -lang=Java -cat=Exp "7 * 12" | linearize -lang=JVM
bipush 7 bipush 12 imul
```

Notice that the Java grammar is ambiguous: `7 * 12 * 9` has two parse trees. GF returns them both and produces two JVM expressions. Allowing ambiguity is one of the first things a natural language grammar has to do. In this very case, however, we would rather eliminate the ambiguity by using precedences, as in Section 2.4.

So let us look at how GF works. The main idea is to separate abstract and concrete syntax. In BNF, these two aspects are expressed together. Thus the BNF rule

```
EMul. Exp ::= Exp "*" Exp
```

says two things at the same time:

- `EMul` is a tree-building function that takes two `Exp` trees and forms an `Exp` tree.

- The tree is linearized to a sequence of tokens where * appears between the expressions.

In GF, these two aspects are expressed by two different rules: a `fun` (function) rule and a `lin` (linearization) rule:

```
fun EMul : Exp -> Exp -> Exp
lin EMul x y = x ++ "*" ++ y
```

The rules are put into separate modules, marked as **abstract** and **concrete**. This makes it possible to combine one **abstract** with several **concretes**, as we did above. Consequently, we can translate by parsing a string in one **concrete**, and linearizing it with another. Notice the concatenation symbol ++, which is needed between tokens; in GF, just writing x "*" y would mean the application of the function x to the arguments "*" and y.

In a BNF grammar, the set of categories is implicit in the sense that there are no separate rules telling what categories there are, but they are collected from the grammar rules. In GF, categories must be introduced explicitly, by cat rules in the abstract and lincat rules in the concrete. The only exception is a handful of predefined categories, such as Int and Float.

The lincat rule specifies the **linearization type** of a category. In the above grammar, it is just Str for Exp in both Java and JVM. But this can be enriched to records, tables, and parameters. Here is a better grammar for Java expressions, taking care of precedence with a parameter:

```
concrete ArithmJava of Arithm = {
  param Prec = P0 | P1 ;
  lincat Exp = {s : Str ; p : Prec} ;
  lin EInt i = {s = i.s ; p = P1} ;
  lin EMul x y = {
    s = x.s ++ "*" ++
        case y.p of {P0 => parenth y.s ; P1 => y.s} ;
    p = P0
    } ;
  oper parenth : Str -> Str = \s -> "(" ++ s ++ ")" ;
  }
```

The grammar defines a **parameter type** (param) called Prec, with two values representing precedence levels 0 and 1. The linearization type of Exp is a **record type**, with a field s for a string and p for a precedence. Integer literals have the higher precedence, and multiplications the lower one. Notice that the built-in type Int also has a record as linearization type, which is shown by the term i.s giving the string field of the record.

The interesting work is done in the linearization rule of EMul. There the second operand gets parentheses if it is an expression on the lower level. The first operand does not, because multiplication is left-associative. The choice is made with a **case** expression, similar to **case** expressions in Haskell. Parentheses are added with the function **parenth**, which is defined as an auxiliary operation (oper).

When parsed with this modified grammar, Java expressions get unique parse trees. The JVM concrete syntax does not need changes. In fact, much of the power of GF comes from the ability to use different linearization types in different languages. In natural languages, parameters are linguistic features such as number, gender, and case. These features work in very different ways depending on language.

Not surprisingly perhaps, GF and BNFC are genetically related. GF was first released in 1998, and it was clear that it could also be used for programming language implementation. However, it was not ideal for this, because the grammar format is too powerful and therefore potentially inefficient, just like the parser combinators of Section 8.6. The idea then arose to create a special version of GF, which uses the much simpler BNF notation and converts the grammars to standard compiler tools. Thus BNFC is a spin-off of GF. As a more powerful formalism, GF is actually able to read grammars written in BNF notation and convert them to GF grammars.

Exercise 8-9. Extend the `Arithm` grammar to cover addition, subtraction, and division. You will now need three precedence levels. To make this nice and modular, you can define an auxiliary operation for left associative infix expressions,

```
oper infixl : Prec -> Str ->
    {s : Str; p : Str} -> {s : Str; p : Str} -> {s : Str; p : Str}
```

which allows you to write

```
lin EAdd = infixl P0 "+" ;
lin EMul = infixl P1 "*" ;
```

and so on.

Exercise 8-10. GF is more powerful than context-free grammars, actually equivalent with **PMCFG (Parallel Multiple Context-Free Grammars)**, with a polynomial worst-case parsing complexity where the exponent is unlimited. The additional power makes it easy to define the **copy language** (Section 3.9). Write a GF grammar for the copy language.

8.12   A GF grammar for queries*

Let us now write a GF grammar for queries in English. We will use yet another feature of GF to make the solution modular and reusable: we use separate modules for basic queries (`Query`) and its application to mathematics (`MathQuery`). The `MathQuery` modules are extensions of `Query`, marked with the symbol ** which roughly corresponds to `extends` of classes in Java.

Abstract syntax

This is the basic query grammar, defining the type system and the forms of queries. Each function is followed by a comment that shows an example that has that structure. Notice the flag `startcat` setting the default start category. Also notice that the keywords `cat` and `fun` need not be repeated in groups of definitions of the same type.

```
abstract Query = {
flags startcat = Query ;
cat
  Query ;
  Kind ;
  Property ;
  Term ;
fun
  QWhich   : Kind -> Property -> Query ;    -- which numbers are prime
  QWhether : Term -> Property -> Query ;    -- is any number prime
  TAll : Kind -> Term ;                     -- all numbers
  TAny : Kind -> Term ;                     -- any number
  PAnd : Property -> Property -> Property ; -- even and prime
  POr  : Property -> Property -> Property ; -- even or odd
  PNot : Property -> Property ;             -- not prime
  KProperty : Property -> Kind -> Kind ;    -- even number
}
```

The `MathQuery` module inherits all categories and functions of `Query` and adds some of its own.

```
abstract MathQuery = Query ** {
fun
  KNumber : Kind ;
  TInteger : Int -> Term ;
  PEven, POdd, PPrime : Property ;
  PDivisible : Term -> Property ;
  PSmaller, PGreater : Term -> Property ;
}
```

English

The BNF grammar for queries in Section 8.10 had two problems, which are easy to solve in GF by parameters. For the different forms of kind expressions, we use a parameter `Number` (in the grammatical sense), with values for the singular (`Sg`) and the plural (`Pl`). The linearization type of `Kind` is a **table type**, `Number => Str`, which is similar to inflection tables in grammars: it gives a string value to each parameter of type `Number`. The linearization of `KNumber` below is an example of a table. The selection operator (`!`) picks values from tables, as exemplified in `QWhich`, `TAll`, and `TAny`. The placement of properties is likewise controlled by a parameter type, `Fix` (prefix or postfix).

```
concrete QueryEng of Query = {
lincat
  Query = Str ;
  Kind = Number => Str ;
  Property = {s : Str ; p : Fix} ;
```

```
    Term = {s : Str ; n : Number} ;
param
    Fix = Pre | Post ;
    Number = Sg | Pl ;
lin
    QWhich kind property = "which" ++ kind ! Pl ++ be ! Pl ++ property.s ;
    QWhether term property = be ! term.n ++ term.s ++ property.s ;
    TAll kind = {s = "all" ++ kind ! Pl ; n = Pl} ;
    TAny kind = {s = "any" ++ kind ! Sg ; n = Sg} ;
    PAnd p q = {s = p.s ++ "and" ++ q.s ; p = fix2 p.p q.p} ;
    POr p q = {s = p.s ++ "or" ++ q.s ; p = fix2 p.p q.p} ;
    PNot p = {s = "not" ++ p.s ; p = Post} ;
    KProperty property kind = \\n => case property.p of {
        Pre  => property.s ++ kind ! n ;
        Post => kind ! n ++ property.s
        } ;
oper
    be : Number => Str = table {Sg => "is" ; Pl => "are"} ;
    prefix : Str -> {s : Str ; p : Fix}  = \s -> {s = s ; p = Pre} ;
    postfix : Str -> {s : Str ; p : Fix} = \s -> {s = s ; p = Post} ;
    fix2 : Fix -> Fix -> Fix = \x,y -> case x of {Post => Post ; _ => y} ;
}

concrete MathQueryEng of MathQuery = QueryEng ** {
lin
    KNumber = table {Sg => "number" ; Pl => "numbers"} ;
    TInteger i = {s = i.s ; n = Sg} ;
    PEven = prefix "even" ;
    POdd = prefix "odd" ;
    PPrime = prefix "prime" ;
    PDivisible term = postfix ("divisible by" ++ term.s) ;
    PSmaller term = postfix ("smaller than" ++ term.s) ;
    PGreater term = postfix ("greater than" ++ term.s) ;
}
```

Exercise 8-11. Apply the query language to some other domain than mathematics.

Exercise 8-12. Extend the query language with new question forms, such as *where* and *when* questions, which may be appropriate for other domains than mathematics.

Exercise 8-13.+ Port the query language to some other language than English, without changing its abstract syntax.

8.13 The answering engine*

Denotational semantics

To interpret the queries, we translate them to predicate logic. Kinds and the top-level *which* queries are interpreted as sets. Top-level *whether* queries are interpreted as formulas, and properties are interpreted as one-place predicates.

The most intricate case is perhaps the interpretation of terms. Plain integer terms could of course be interpreted as integers. But this would not work for *all* and *any* terms, which are more like quantifiers in logic. To make this work, we interpret all terms as functions that take predicates as arguments! For *all* and *any*, this works in the natural way. For integer terms, this creates a rather indirect interpretation, which is a function that for any predicate p applies that predicate to the given integer i.

The interpretation is an example of yet another kind of programming language semantics, known as **denotational semantics**. It uses syntax-directed translation to define the operator $*$ which specifies the **denotation** (the meaning) of each syntax tree.

$$(QWhich\ kind\ prop)^* = \{x | x \in kind^*, prop^*(x)\}$$
$$(QWhether\ term\ prop)^* = term^*(prop^*)$$
$$(TAll\ kind)^* = \lambda p.(\forall x)(x \in kind^* \supset p(x))$$
$$(TAny\ kind)^* = \lambda p.(\exists x)(x \in kind^* \& p(x))$$
$$(TAnd\ p\ q)^* = \lambda x.p^*(x)\& q^*(x)$$
$$(TOr\ p\ q)^* = \lambda x.p^*(x) \vee q^*(x)$$
$$(TNot\ p)^* = \lambda x. \sim p^*(x)$$
$$(KProperty\ prop\ kind)^* = \{x | x \in kind^*, prop^*(x)\}$$
$$(TInteger\ i)^* = \lambda p.p^*(i)$$

The predicates of `MathQuery` can easily be given some adequate interpretations.

Denotational semantics is often a natural choice for interpreting declarative languages. In fact, we used a variant of it in Section 3.2, when interpreting regular expressions as formal languages. There we used a double bracket notation instead of the more compact asterisk.

Compiling to Haskell

The concrete syntax in GF is actually also an example of denotational semantics! It is an interpretation of syntax trees as strings, records, and tables. We can use this idea to give an implementation of the query language as translation to Haskell code. In Haskell, we will use lists rather than sets as denotations of kinds. But otherwise the translation is very much the same as the denotational semantics.

```
concrete QueryHs of Query = {
lincat
  Query, Kind, Property, Term, Element = Str ;
lin
  QWhich kind prop = "[x | x <-" ++ kind ++ "," ++ prop ++ "x" ++ "]" ;
  QWhether term prop = term ++ prop ;
  TAll kind = parenth ("\\p -> and [p x | x <-" ++ kind ++ ", p x]") ;
  TAny kind = parenth ("\\p -> or  [p x | x <-" ++ kind ++ ", p x]") ;
  PAnd p q = parenth ("\\x ->" ++ p ++ "x &&" ++ q ++ "x") ;
  POr p q = parenth ("\\x ->" ++ p ++ "x ||" ++ q ++ "x") ;
  PNot p = parenth ("\\x -> not" ++ parenth (p ++ "x")) ;
  KProperty prop kind = "[x | x <-" ++ kind ++ "," ++ prop ++ "x" ++ "]" ;
oper
  parenth : Str -> Str = \s -> "(" ++ s ++ ")" ;
}


concrete MathQueryHs of MathQuery = QueryHs ** {
lin
  KNumber = "[0 .. 1000]" ;
  TInteger i = parenth ("\\p -> p" ++ i.s) ;
  PEven = "even" ;
  POdd = "odd" ;
  PPrime = parenth ("\\x -> x > 1 && all (\\y -> mod x y /=0) [2..div x 2]") ;
  PDivisible e = parenth ("\\x ->" ++ e ++ parenth ("\\y -> mod x y == 0")) ;
  PSmaller e = parenth ("\\x ->" ++ e ++ parenth ("x<")) ;
  PGreater e = parenth ("\\x ->" ++ e ++ parenth ("x>")) ;
}
```

Of course, we could make the generated Haskell code nicer by using precedences
to eliminate some parentheses, as shown in Section 8.11. But this is not so
important, because we use Haskell only internally, as question answering engine.
We set an upper bound 1000 for numbers to prevent infinite search. Here is an
example of a query and its translation as obtained in the GF shell:

```
> p -lang=Eng "which even numbers are prime" | l -lang=Hs
[x | x <- [x | x <- [0 .. 1000] , even x ] ,
  ( \x -> x > 1 && all (\y -> mod x y /=0) [2..div x 2] ) x ]
```

We can thus translate queries from English to Haskell in GF. As the simplest
possible end-user interface, we can write a shell script **query**, which pipes the
English query to GF, which produces a Haskell translation, which is sent to the
GHC Haskell compiler. The flag **-e** makes GHC work as an expression interpreter. The GF command **pt -number=1** makes sure that just one expression
is sent to Haskell, if the parse happens to be ambiguous.

```
#!/bin/bash
```

```
ghc -e "$(echo "p -lang=Eng \"$1\" | pt -number=1 \
   | l -lang=Hs" | gf -run MathQueryEng.gf MathQueryHs.gf)"
```

Now the user interaction may look as follows:

```
./query "is any even number prime"
True
```

```
./query "which numbers greater than 100 and smaller than 150 are prime"
[101,103,107,109,113,127,131,137,139,149]
```

8.14   The limits of grammars*

Even though GF is expressive enough for natural language grammars, they can require substantial work and expertise. To make this work easier, GF has a Resource Grammar Library, which implements low-level linguistic details of different languages, such as inflection and word order, and makes them accessible by a high-level API. For example, kinds can be implemented as common nouns (CN), properties as adjectives (A), and KProperty with the funtion mkCN, which combines an adjective with a common noun:

```
lincat Kind = CN ;
lincat Property = A ;
lin KProperty prop kind = mkCN prop kind ;
```

The same definitions work for all of the currently 24 languages of the library, although for instance the order of the adjective and the noun can vary in concrete syntax (*even number* in English becomes *nombre pair* in French). Differences of course also appear on the level of words, where mkA in each language produces an adjective inflection table:

```
PEven = mkA "even"        -- English
PEven = mkA "parillinen"  -- Finnish
pEven = mkA "pair"        -- French
PEven = mkA "gerade"      -- German
```

English needs only one form of adjectives, but French has 4 and Finnish over 30.

GF makes it possible to generate and parse natural languages, whenever the sentences involved are within the scope of a grammar. What is out of reach, however, is the parsing of the *whole* natural language. The problem is that, in natural language, the grammar is not something that can be given once and for all. This is in contrast to programming languages, which are *defined* by their grammars. For natural language, the grammar is more like an open research problem, and the language can change at any time.

Nevertheless, it is instructive to compare natural language processing with compilation. Many compilation phases have counterparts in machine translation:

- **Lexical analysis**: recognize and classify words.

- **Parsing**: build an abstract syntax tree.

- **Semantic analysis**: disambiguate; add information to tree.

- **Generation**: linearize to target language.

Lexical analysis, parsing, and generation are in both cases derived from grammars, even though grammars are typically much harder to write for natural languages than for programming languages. But what about semantic analysis?

In compilers, semantic analysis usually requires more work than the other phases. There are two reasons for this. First, the grammars are usually easy, since computer languages are simple. Secondly, there is often a considerable **semantic gap** between the source and target languages, which requires substantial analysis and maybe restructuring the tree. For instance, type information may need to be added, and variables may need to be converted to memory addresses or registers.

In natural language translation, writing the grammars can itself be a substantial task. On the other hand, the semantic gap between natural languages is typically not so huge as between high-level programming languages and machine languages. This is illustrated by the GF resource grammar library, which implements the same structures for many languages. As long as these structures are preserved in translation, all that is needed is just to select proper words in the target language to fill in the structures.

However, when parsing natural language, semantic analysis problems due to **ambiguity** soon arise. A typical example is **word sense disambiguation**: one word may have several possible translations, corresponding to different meanings of the word. For instance, the English word *drug* is in French *médicament* (medical drug) or *drogue* (narcotic drug). The proper translation of

> the company produces drugs against malaria

is in most cases

> la société produit des médicaments contre le paludisme

because substances used against malaria are medical drugs, not narcotic drugs. Notice the similarity of this analysis to **overload resolution** in compilers (Section 4.6): to translate Java's + into JVM, it is necessary to find out the types of its operands, and then select either `iadd` or `dadd` or string concatenation.

Ambiguity extends from words to syntactic structures. Consider the sentences

> *I ate a pizza with shrimps*
>
> *I ate a pizza with friends*

The phrases *with shrimps* and *with friends* can attach to the noun *pizza* but also to the whole act of eating. The preposition chosen in French translation depends on this, and so does indeed the meaning of the sentence. Again, by using our knowledge about what things can go together, we can guess that the following analyses are correct:

> *I ate a (pizza with shrimps)*
>
> *(I ate a pizza) with friends*

Syntactic ambiguity is a problem that programming languages mostly avoid by design. But we have already seen an exception: the dangling else problem (Section 3.8). It *is* a real ambiguity in the grammar, but it is avoided by an *ad hoc* rule forcing one of the parses. Another example is the type cast syntax of C++, which creates an ambiguity between function declarations and object declarations with casts:

```
char *aName(String(s));
```

This ambiguity is resolved by a complex rule stating that, whatever can be interpreted as a function declaration, is a function declaration.

Ambiguity is no problem for grammars as such: the parser can simply return all trees, and the problem is transferred to the semantic analysis level. What can be a problem in practice is the high number of trees. For instance, the phrase

> *pizza with shrimps from waters without salt from countries in Asia*

can syntactically have 42 analyses, and their number grows exponentially in the number of attachments.

Another problem in natural language parsing is **parse error recovery**. A compiler may expect the programmer to obey the grammar published in the language manual and simply report a syntax error if a program can't be parsed. But no such manual exists for natural languages. Therefore a system should rather be **robust**: it should recover from errors by using some back-up method. (An alternative is **predictive parsing**, which helps the user to stick to the grammar by giving suggestions. But this is only viable in interactive systems, not in batch-oriented text parsers.)

A popular solution to both error recovery and disambiguation is to use **statistical language models**, i.e. data about the co-occurrences of words and sequences of words. Disambiguation can for instance use the fact that *drogues contre le paludisme* is less common than *médicaments contre le paludisme*. And error recovery can use **smoothing**: if a sought-for sequence of three words *u v w* cannot be found in the model, it can perhaps be combined from two sequences of two words, *u v* and *v w*.

The choice between grammar-based and statistical methods often depends on the purpose. There is a basic trade-off between **coverage** and **precision** in natural language processing. Systems like Google translate want to deal with any user input and therefore opt for coverage; no grammar could do this in a useful way. Systems like voice commands in a car deal with limited domains of language, but have to do this with precision. In such applications, one can use small languages defined by grammars, as our query language above.

But even in large-scale natural language translation, the main current trend is to bring in more grammatical information to statistical systems to improve their quality. The result is called **hybrid systems**. Interestingly, combinations of rules and statistics are also increasingly used in compilers, as a response to unsolvable problems such as optimization (Section 6.11), or to problems whose rule-based solutions are too complex in practice.

An example is register allocation, where a notion of **spilling cost** is used for deciding which variables to spill, that is, not to store in registers. The cost is estimated by statistics on their usage, with heuristics such as giving a higher cost to variables occurring in loops. The simplest way to do this is by counting occurrences in the code at compile time. But one can also take a step further and use **profiling**—the analysis on actual runs of programs. Thus GCC has options for running a program in a mode that collects statistics and using the outcome in later compilations of the same program. Profiling can for instance tell how many times different branches were taken, which may be impossible to know from the program code alone.

However, compiler construction is much more cautious in its use of statistics than natural language processing. Anything that affects the semantics of programs is based on firm knowledge and rules; statistics is just used as a possible source of extra gain such as speed improvement.

Exercise 8-14. Is the English query grammar ambiguous? Do the ambiguities affect the semantics, that is, what answers are given? One way to test ambiguity is to let GF randomly generate trees, linearize them, and parse them back to see if there are several results:

```
> generate_random | lin -tr | parse
```

Appendix A

BNFC Quick Reference

by Markus Forsberg and Aarne Ranta

This Appendix is based on the *LBNF Report* by Forsberg and Ranta, and some documentation by Ulf Norell. The sources are available on the BNFC web page,

    http://bnfc.digitalgrammars.com

A.1   The BNFC tool

BNFC is a single-source multi-target tool for compiler construction. It reads a single file, a grammar in **Labelled BNF** (**LBNF**), and produces a set of modules in a chosen host language. The following diagram shows the available host languages and the components produced in all of them.

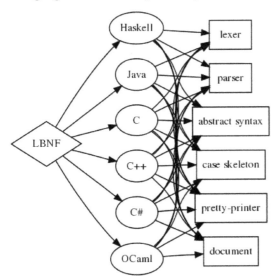

This document describes the syntax and semantics of LBNF. It corresponds to BNFC Version 2.5, which will be kept available via the book web page even when later versions appear.

A.2   Overview of LBNF

An LBNF grammar is a BNF grammar where every rule is given a label. The label is used for constructing a syntax tree whose subtrees are given by the nonterminals of the rule, in the same order. For example, the rule

```
SWhile. Stm ::= "while" "(" Exp ")" Stm ;
```

has the label SWhile and forms trees of the form (SWhile e s), where e is a tree for Exp and s a tree for Stm.

More formally, an LBNF grammar consists of a collection of rules, which have the following form (expressed by a regular expression; Section A.9 gives a complete BNF definition of the notation):

Ident "." Ident "::=" (Ident | String)* ";" ;

The first identifier is the **rule label**, followed by the **value category**. On the right-hand side of the production arrow (::=) is the list of production items. An item is either a quoted string (**terminal**) or a category symbol (**nonterminal**). The right-hand side of a rule whose value category is C is called a **production** for C.

Identifiers, that is, rule names and category symbols, can be chosen *ad libitum*, with the restrictions imposed by the target language. To satisfy Haskell, and C and Java as well, the following rule should be followed with rule labels and categories:

> An identifier is a nonempty sequence of letters, digits, and under-scores, starting with a capital letter.

Additional features

Basic LBNF as defined above is clearly sufficient for defining any context-free language. However, it is not always convenient to define a programming language purely with BNF rules. Therefore, some additional features are added to LBNF: abstract syntax conventions, lexer rules, pragmas, and macros. These features are treated in the subsequent sections.

Abstract syntax conventions. Creating an abstract syntax by adding a node type for every BNF rule may sometimes become too detailed, or cluttered with extra structural levels. To remedy this, we have identified the most common problem cases, and added to LBNF some extra conventions to handle them.

Lexer rules. Some aspects of a language belong to its lexical structure rather than its grammar, and are more naturally described by regular expressions than by BNF rules. We have therefore added to LBNF two rule formats to define the lexical structure: **tokens** and **comments**.

Pragmas. Pragmas are rules instructing the BNFC grammar compiler to treat some rules of the grammar in certain special ways: to reduce the number of **entrypoints** or to treat some syntactic forms as **internal** only.

Macros. Macros are syntactic sugar for potentially large groups of rules and help to write grammars concisely. This is both for the writer's and the reader's convenience; among other things, macros naturally force certain groups of rules to go together, which could otherwise be spread arbitrarily in the grammar.

Layout syntax. This is a non-context-free feature present in some programming languages, such as Haskell and Python. LBNF has a set of rule formats for defining a limited form of layout syntax. It works as a preprocessor that translates layout syntax into explicit structure markers.

Semantic definitions. Some labels can be excluded from the final abstract syntax by rules that define them in terms of other labels.

A.3   Abstract syntax conventions

Predefined basic types

The first convention are predefined basic types. Basic types, such as integer and character, could of course be defined in a labelled BNF, for example:

```
Char_a. Char ::= "a" ;
Char_b. Char ::= "b" ;
```

This is, however, cumbersome and inefficient. Instead, we have decided to extend our formalism with predefined basic types, and represent their grammar as a part of lexical structure. These types are the following, as defined by LBNF regular expressions (see below for the regular expression syntax):

- `Integer` of integers, defined

    ```
    digit+
    ```

- `Double` of floating point numbers, defined

    ```
    digit+ '.' digit+ ('e' '-'? digit+)?
    ```

- `Char` of characters (in single quotes), defined

  ```
  '\'' ((char-["'\\"]) | ('\\' ["'\\nt"])) '\''
  ```

- `String` of strings (in double quotes), defined

  ```
  '"' ((char-["\"\\"]) | ('\\' ["\"\\nt"]))* '"'
  ```

- `Ident` of identifiers, defined

  ```
  letter (letter | digit | '_' | '\'')*
  ```

In the abstract syntax, these types are represented as corresponding types of each language, except `Ident`, for which no such type exists. It is treated by a `newtype` in Haskell,

```
newtype Ident = Ident String
```

as `String` in Java, and as a `typedef` to `char*` in C and `string` in C++.

As the names of the types suggest, the lexer produces high-precision variants, for integers and floats. Authors of applications can truncate these numbers later if they want to have low precision instead.

Predefined categories may not have explicit productions in the grammar, since this would violate their predefined meanings.

Semantic dummies

Sometimes the concrete syntax of a language includes rules that make no semantic difference. An example is a BNF rule making the parser accept extra semicolons after statements:

```
Stm ::= Stm ";" ;
```

As this rule is semantically dummy, we do not want to represent it by a constructors in the abstract syntax. Instead, we introduce the following convention:

> A rule label can be an underscore _, which does not add anything to the syntax tree.

Thus we can write the following rule in LBNF:

```
_ . Stm ::= Stm ";" ;
```

Underscores are of course only meaningful as replacements of one-argument constructors where the value type is the same as the argument type. Semantic dummies leave no trace in the pretty-printer. Thus, for instance, the pretty-printer "normalizes away" extra semicolons.

Precedence levels

A common idiom in (ordinary) BNF is to use indexed variants of categories to express precedence levels:

```
Exp2 ::= Integer ;
Exp1 ::= Exp1 "*" Exp2 ;
Exp  ::= Exp  "+" Exp1 ;
Exp  ::= Exp1 ;
Exp1 ::= Exp2 ;
Exp2 ::= "(" Exp ")" ;
```

The precedence level regulates the order of parsing, including associativity. Parentheses lift an expression of any level to the highest level.

A straightforward labelling of the above rules creates a grammar that does have the desired recognition behavior, as the abstract syntax is cluttered with type distinctions (between Exp, Exp2, and Exp3) and constructors (from the last three rules) with no semantic content. The BNF Converter solution is to distinguish among category symbols those that are just indexed variants of each other:

> A category symbol can end with an integer index (i.e. a sequence of digits), and is then treated as a type synonym of the corresponding non-indexed symbol.

Thus Exp1 and Exp2 are indexed variants of Exp. The plain Exp is a synonym of Exp0.

Transitions between indexed variants are semantically dummy, and we do not want to represent them by constructors in the abstract syntax. To do this, we extend the use of underscores to indexed variants. The example grammar above can now be labelled as follows:

```
EInt.   Exp2 ::= Integer ;
ETimes. Exp1 ::= Exp1 "*" Exp2 ;
EPlus.  Exp  ::= Exp  "+" Exp1 ;
_.           Exp  ::= Exp1 ;
_.           Exp1 ::= Exp2 ;
_.           Exp2 ::= "(" Exp ")" ;
```

In Haskell, for instance, the data type of expressions becomes simply

```
data Exp = EInt Integer | ETimes Exp Exp | EPlus Exp Exp
```

and the syntax tree for 5*(6+7) is

```
ETimes (EInt 5) (EPlus (EInt 6) (EInt 7))
```

Indexed categories *can* be used for other purposes than precedence, since the
only thing we can formally check is the type skeleton (see the Section A.3). The
parser does not need to know that the indices mean precedence, but only that
indexed variants have values of the same type. The pretty-printer, however,
assumes that indexed categories are used for precedence, and may produce
strange results if they are used in some other way.

Polymorphic lists

It is easy to define monomorphic list types in LBNF:

```
NilDef.  ListDef ::= ;
ConsDef. ListDef ::= Def ";" ListDef ;
```

However, compiler writers in languages like Haskell may want to use predefined
polymorphic lists, because of the language support for these constructs. LBNF
permits the use of Haskell's list constructors as labels, and list brackets in
category names:

```
[].  [Def] ::= ;
(:). [Def] ::= Def ";" [Def] ;
```

As the general rule, we have

   $[C]$, the category of lists of type C,

   [] and (:), the Nil and Cons rule labels,

   (:[]), the rule label for one-element lists.

The third rule label is used to place an at-least-one restriction, but also to
permit special treatment of one-element lists in the concrete syntax.

   In the LATEX document (for stylistic reasons) and in the Happy file (for
syntactic reasons), the category name [X] is replaced by ListX. In order for
this not to cause clashes, ListX may not be at the same time used explicitly
in the grammar.

   The list category constructor can be iterated: [[X]], [[[X]]], etc behave
in the expected way.

   The list notation can also be seen as a variant of the Kleene star and plus,
and hence as an ingredient from Extended BNF.

An optimization: left-recursive lists

The BNF representation of lists is right-recursive, following the list constructor
in Haskell and most other languages. Right-recursive lists, however, are an
inefficient way of parsing lists in an LALR parser, because they can blow up
the stack size. The smart programmer would implement a pair of rules such as

```
[].     [Stm] ::= ;
(:).    [Stm] ::= Stm ";" [Stm] ;
```

not in the direct way, but under a left-recursive transformation, as if we wrote,

```
[].          [Stm] ::= ;
(flip (:)). [Stm] ::= [Stm] Stm ";" ;
```

Then the smart programmer would also be careful to **reverse** the list when it is used as an argument of another rule construction.

The BNF Converter automatically performs the left-recursion transformation for pairs of rules of the form

```
[].  [C] ::= ;
(:). [C] ::= C x [C] ;
```

where C is any category and x is any sequence of terminals (possibly empty). These rules are also generated from the **terminator** macro (Section A.6).

Notice. The transformation is currently not performed if the one-element list is the base case.

The type-correctness of LBNF rules

It is customary in parser generators to delegate the checking of certain errors to the target language. For instance, a Happy source file that Happy processes without complaints can still produce a Haskell file that is rejected by Haskell. In the same way, the BNF converter delegates some checking to the generated language (for instance, the parser conflict check). However, since it is always the easiest for the programmer to understand error messages related to the source, the BNF Converter performs some checks, which are mostly connected with the sanity of the abstract syntax.

The type checker uses a notion of the *category skeleton* of a rule, which is a pair

$$(C, A \ldots B)$$

where C is the unindexed left-hand-side nonterminal and $A \ldots B$ is the sequence of unindexed right-hand-side nonterminals of the rule. In other words, the category skeleton of a rule expresses the abstract-syntax type of the semantic action associated to that rule.

We also need the notions of a *regular category* and a *regular rule label*. Briefly, regular labels and categories are the user-defined ones. More formally, a regular category is none of [C],Integer, Double, Char, String and Ident, or the types defined by **token** rules (Section A.4). A regular rule label is none of _, [], (:), and (:[]).

The type checking rules are now the following:

A rule labelled by _ must have a category skeleton of form (C, C).

A rule labelled by [] must have a category skeleton of form $([C],)$.

A rule labelled by (:) must have a category skeleton of form $([C], C[C])$.

A rule labelled by (:[]) must have a category skeleton of form $([C], C)$.

Only regular categories may have productions with regular rule labels.

Every regular category occurring in the grammar must have at least one production with a regular rule label.

All rules with the same regular rule label must have the same category skeleton.

The second-last rule corresponds to the absence of empty data types in Haskell. The last rule could be strengthened so as to require that all regular rule labels be unique: this is needed to guarantee error-free pretty-printing. Violating this strengthened rule currently generates only a warning, not a type error.

A.4   Lexer Definitions

The token rule

The token rule enables the LBNF programmer to define new lexical types using a simple regular expression notation. For instance, the following rule defines the type of identifiers beginning with upper-case letters.

```
token UIdent (upper (letter | digit | ’_’)*) ;
```

The type UIdent becomes usable as an LBNF nonterminal and as a type in the abstract syntax. Each token type is implemented by a newtype in Haskell, as a String in Java, and as a typedef to char* in C/C++.

The regular expression syntax of LBNF is specified in Section A.9. The abbreviations with strings in brackets need a word of explanation:

["abc7%"] denotes the union of the characters ’a’ ’b’ ’c’ ’7’ ’%’

{"abc7%"} denotes the sequence of the characters ’a’ ’b’ ’c’ ’7’ ’%’

The atomic expressions upper, lower, letter, and digit denote the character classes suggested by their names (letters are isolatin1). The expression char matches any character in the 8-bit ASCII range, and the "epsilon" expression `eps` matches the empty string.[1] Thus `eps` is equivalent to `{""}`, whereas the empty language is expressed by `[""]`.

Note. The empty language is not available for the Java lexer tool JLex.

The `position token` rule

Any `token` rule can be modified by the word `position`, which has the effect that the data type defined will carry position information. For instance,

```
position token PIdent (letter (letter|digit|'_'|'\'')*) ;
```

creates in Haskell the data type definition

```
newtype PIdent = PIdent ((Int,Int),String)
```

where the pair of integers indicates the line and column of the first character of the token. The pretty-printer omits the position component.

The `comment` rule

Comments are segments of source code that include free text and are not passed to the parser. The natural place to deal with them is in the lexer. The `comment` rule instructs the lexer generator to treat certain pieces of text as comments.

The comment rule takes one or two string arguments. The first string defines how a comment begins. The second, optional string marks the end of a comment; if it is not given then the comment is ended by a newline. For instance, the Java comment convention is defined as follows:

```
comment "//" ;
comment "/*" "*/" ;
```

A.5 Pragmas

Internal pragmas

Sometimes we want to include in the abstract syntax structures that are not part of the concrete syntax, and hence not parsable. They can be, for instance, syntax trees that are produced by a type-annotating type checker. Even though they are not parsable, we may want to pretty-print them, for instance, in the type checker's error messages. To define such an internal constructor, we use a pragma

```
"internal" Rule ";"
```

---

[1] If we want to describe full Java or Haskell, we must extend the character set to Unicode. This is currently not supported by all lexer tools, however.

where `Rule` is a normal LBNF rule. For instance,

```
internal EVarT. Exp ::= "(" Ident ":" Type ")";
```

introduces a type-annotated variant of a variable expression.

Entry point pragmas

The BNF Converter generates, by default, a parser for every category in the grammar. This is unnecessarily rich in most cases, and makes the parser larger than needed. If the size of the parser becomes critical, the *entry points pragma* enables the user to define which of the parsers are actually exported:

```
entrypoints (Ident ",")* Ident ;
```

For instance, the following pragma defines `Stm` and `Exp` to be the only entry points:

```
entrypoints Stm, Exp ;
```

A.6   Macros

Terminators and separators

The `terminator` macro defines a pair of list rules by what token terminates each element in the list. For instance,

```
terminator Stm ";" ;
```

tells that each statement (`Stm`) in a list `[Stm]` is terminated with a semicolon (`;`). It is a shorthand for the pair of rules

```
[].   [Stm] ::= ;
(:).  [Stm] ::= Stm ";" [Stm] ;
```

The qualifier `nonempty` in the macro makes one-element list to be the base case. Thus

```
terminator nonempty Stm ";" ;
```

is shorthand for

```
(:[]). [Stm] ::= Stm ";" ;
(:).   [Stm] ::= Stm ";" [Stm] ;
```

The terminator can be specified as empty `""`. No token is introduced then, but e.g.

```
terminator Stm "" ;
```

is translated to

```
[].   [Stm] ::= ;
(:).  [Stm] ::= Stm [Stm] ;
```

The `separator` macro is similar to `terminator`, except that the separating token is not attached to the last element. Thus

```
separator Stm ";" ;
```

means

```
[].      [Stm] ::= ;
(:[]).   [Stm] ::= Stm ;
(:).     [Stm] ::= Stm ";" [Stm] ;
```

whereas

```
separator nonempty Stm ";" ;
```

means

```
(:[]).   [Stm] ::= Stm ;
(:).     [Stm] ::= Stm ";" [Stm] ;
```

Notice that, if the empty token `""` is used, there is no difference between `terminator` and `separator`.

Note. The grammar generated from a `separator` without `nonempty` will actually also accept a list terminating with a semicolon, whereas the pretty-printer "normalizes" it away. This might be considered a bug, but a set of rules forbidding the terminating semicolon would be much more complicated. The `nonempty` case is precise.

Coercions

The `coercions` macro is a shorthand for a group of rules translating between precedence levels. For instance,

```
coercions Exp 3 ;
```

is shorthand for

```
_. Exp   ::= Exp1 ;
_. Exp1  ::= Exp2 ;
_. Exp2  ::= Exp3 ;
_. Exp3  ::= "(" Exp ")" ;
```

Because of the total coverage of these coercions, it does not matter if the integer indicating the highest level (here 3) is bigger than the highest level actually occurring, or if there are some other levels without productions in the grammar.

Unlabelled rules

The `rules` macro is a shorthand for a set of rules from which labels are generated automatically. For instance,

```
rules Type ::= Type "[" Integer "]" | "float" | "int" | Type "*" ;
```

is shorthand for

```
Type_0.     Type ::= Type "[" Integer "]" ;
Type_float. Type ::= "float" ;
Type_int.   Type ::= "int" ;
Type_3.     Type ::= Type "*" ;
```

The labels are created automatically. A label starts with the value category name. If the production has just one item, which is moreover possible as a part of an identifier, that item is used as a suffix. In other cases, an integer suffix is used. No global checks are performed when generating these labels. Any label name clashes that result from them are captured by BNFC type checking on the generated rules.

Notice that, using the `rules` macro, it is possible to define an LBNF grammar without giving any labels. To guarantee the uniqueness of labels, the productions of each category should then be grouped together.

A.7   Semantic definitions

(Section based on BNFC documentation by Ulf Norell.)

LBNF gives support for syntax tree constructors that are eliminated during parsing, by following **semantic definitions**. Here is an example: a core statement language, where we use capital initials to indicate that they will be preserved:

```
Assign. Stm ::= Ident "=" Exp ;
Block.  Stm ::= "{" [Stm] "}" ;
While.  Stm ::= "while" "(" Exp ")" Stm ;
If.     Stm ::= "if" "(" Exp ")" Stm "else" Stm ;
```

We now want to have some syntactic sugar. Note that the labels for these rules all start with a lowercase letter, indicating that they correspond to defined functions rather than nodes in the abstract syntax tree.

```
if.   Stm ::= "if" "(" Exp ")" Stm "endif" ;
for.  Stm ::= "for" "(" Stm ";" Exp ";" Stm ")" Stm ;
inc.  Stm ::= Ident "++" ;
```

Functions are defined using the **define** keyword. Definitions have the form

$$\text{define } f \; x_1 \; \ldots \; x_n \; = \; e$$

where e is an expression on applicative form using the variables $x_1, \ldots, x_n$, other rule labels, lists, and literals.

```
define if e s       = If e s (Block []) ;
define for i c s b  = Block [i, While c (Block [b, s])] ;
define inc x        = Assign x (EOp (EVar x) Plus (EInt 1)) ;
```

Another use of defined functions is to simplify the abstract syntax for binary operators. Instead of one node for each operator one can have a general node (EOp) for all binary operator applications.

```
_. Op ::= Op1;
_. Op ::= Op2;

Less.  Op1 ::= "<";
Equal. Op1 ::= "==";
Plus.  Op2 ::= "+" ;
Minus. Op2 ::= "-" ;

op.    Exp  ::= Exp1 Op1 Exp1 ;
op.    Exp1 ::= Exp1 Op2 Exp2 ;
EInt.  Exp2 ::= Integer ;
EVar.  Exp2 ::= Ident ;
```

Precedence levels can be used to make sure that the pretty printer prints enough parenthesis.

```
internal EOp. Exp ::= Exp2 Op Exp2 ;
define op e1 o e2 = EOp e1 o e2 ;
coercions Exp 2;
```

A.8 Layout syntax

Layout syntax is a means of using indentation to group program elements. It is used in some languages, e.g. Haskell. Those who do not know what layout syntax is or who do not like it can skip this section.

The pragmas **layout**, **layout stop**, and **layout toplevel** define a **layout syntax** for a language. Before these pragmas were added, layout syntax was not definable in BNFC. The layout pragmas are only available for the files generated for Haskell-related tools; if Java, C, or C++ programmers want

to handle layout, they can use the Haskell layout resolver as a preprocessor
to their front end, before the lexer. In Haskell, the layout resolver appears,
automatically, in its most natural place, which is between the lexer and the
parser. The layout pragmas of BNFC are not powerful enough to handle the
full layout rule of Haskell 98, but they suffice for the "regular" cases.

Here is an example, found in the the grammar of the logical framework Alfa
(a predecessor of Agda):

```
layout "of", "let", "where", "sig", "struct" ;
```

The first line says that `"of"`, `"let"`, `"where"`, `"sig"`, `"struct"` are *layout
words*, i.e. start a *layout list*. A layout list is a list of expressions normally
enclosed in curly brackets and separated by semicolons, as shown by the Alfa
example

```
ECase. Exp ::= "case" Exp "of" "{" [Branch] "}" ;
```

```
separator Branch ";" ;
```

When the layout resolver finds the token `of` in the code (i.e. in the sequence
of its lexical tokens), it checks if the next token is an opening curly bracket.
If it is, nothing special is done until a layout word is encountered again. The
parser will expect the semicolons and the closing bracket to appear as usual.

But, if the token t following `of` is not an opening curly bracket, a bracket
is inserted, and the start column of t is remembered as the position at which
the elements of the layout list must begin. Semicolons are inserted at those
positions. When a token is eventually encountered left of the position of t (or
end-of-file reached), a closing bracket is inserted at that point.

Nested layout blocks are allowed, which means that the layout resolver
maintains a stack of positions. Pushing a position on the stack corresponds to
inserting a left bracket, and popping from the stack corresponds to inserting a
right bracket.

Here is an example of an Alfa source file using layout:

```
c :: Nat = case x of
  True -> b
  False -> case y of
    False -> b
  Neither -> d

d = case x of True -> case y of False -> g
                                x -> b
              y -> h
```

Here is what it looks like after layout resolution:

```
c :: Nat = case x of {
  True -> b
  ;False -> case y of {
    False -> b
  };Neither -> d

};d = case x of {True -> case y of {False -> g
                                    ;x -> b
              };y -> h} ;
```

There are two more layout-related pragmas. The `layout stop` pragma, as in

```
layout stop "in" ;
```

tells the resolver that the layout list can be exited with some stop words, like in, which exits a `let` list. It is no error in the resolver to exit some other kind of layout list with `in`, but an error will show up in the parser.

The

```
layout toplevel ;
```

pragma tells that the whole source file is a layout list, even though no layout word indicates this. The position is the first column, and the resolver adds a semicolon after every paragraph whose first token is at this position. No curly brackets are added. The Alfa file above is an example of this, with two such semicolons added.

To make layout resolution a stand-alone program, e.g. to serve as a preprocessor, the programmer can modify the BNFC-generated file (`LayoutX.hs` for the language `X`) and either compile it or run it in the GHCi interpreter by

```
runghc LayoutX.hs <X-source-file>
```

Note. The generated layout resolver does not work correctly if a layout word is the first token on a line.

A.9   The BNF grammar of LBNF

This document is a slightly modified version of the language document automatically generated by the BNF Converter. We have omitted some experimental and obsolete constructs and reformulated some explanations. But except for the omitted rules, the definitions of lexical and syntactic structure are retained as generated. This guarantees that the BNFC-generated lexer, parser, and abstract syntax are in synchrony with this document.

The lexical structure of LBNF

Identifiers, `Ident`, are unquoted strings beginning with a letter, followed by any combination of letters, digits, and the characters _ and '. Reserved words are excluded from identifiers.

String literals,`String`, have the form `"x"`, where x is any sequence of any characters except " unless preceded by \.

Integer literals, `Integer`, are nonempty sequences of digits.

Character literals `Char` have the form `'c'`, where c is any single character.

Float literals, `Double`, have the structure of two sequences of digits separated by a decimal point, optionally followed by an unsigned or negative exponent marked with an **e**.

Reserved words are the terminals appearing in the grammar. Those reserved words that consist of non-letter characters are called symbols, and they are treated in a different way from those that are similar to identifiers. The lexer follows rules familiar from languages like Haskell, C, and Java, including longest match and spacing conventions.

The reserved words used in BNF are the following:

char	coercions	comment	define	digit	entrypoints
eps	internal	layout	letter	lower	nonempty
position	rules	separator	stop	terminator	token
toplevel	upper	views			

The symbols used in BNF are the following:

$$: \quad ; \quad . \quad ::= \quad [\ ] \quad \_ \quad (\ )$$
$$, \quad = \quad | \quad - \quad * \quad + \quad ? \quad \{ \ \}$$

Comments. End-of-line comments begin with `--`. Comments of any length are enclosed with `{-` and `-}`.

The syntactic structure of LBNF

In the following specification, nonterminals are shown in italics, terminals in type-writer font. The symbols ::= (production), | (union), and ϵ (empty right-hand side) belong to the BNF notation.

LGrammar	::=	ListLDef
LDef	::=	Def
	|	ListIdent : Def
	|	views ListIdent
ListLDef	::=	ε
	|	LDef
	|	LDef ; ListLDef
Grammar	::=	ListDef
ListDef	::=	ε
	|	Def
	|	Def ; ListDef
ListItem	::=	ε
	|	Item ListItem
Def	::=	Label . Cat ::= ListItem
	|	comment String
	|	comment String String
	|	internal Label . Cat ::= ListItem
	|	token Ident Reg
	|	position token Ident Reg
	|	entrypoints ListIdent
	|	separator MinimumSize Cat String
	|	terminator MinimumSize Cat String
	|	coercions Ident Integer
	|	rules Ident ::= ListRHS
	|	define Ident ListArg = Exp
	|	layout ListString
	|	layout stop ListString
	|	layout toplevel
Item	::=	String
	|	Cat
Cat	::=	[Cat]
	|	Ident
Label	::=	Ident
	|	-
	|	[ ]
	|	(:)
	|	(: [ ])
Arg	::=	Ident
ListArg	::=	ε
	|	Arg ListArg
Exp	::=	Exp1 : Exp
	|	Exp1

Exp1	::=	*Ident ListExp2*
	|	*Exp2*
Exp2	::=	*Ident*
	|	*Integer*
	|	*Char*
	|	*String*
	|	*Double*
	|	[*ListExp*]
	|	(*Exp*)
ListExp2	::=	*Exp2*
	|	*Exp2 ListExp2*
ListExp	::=	ϵ
	|	*Exp*
	|	*Exp* , *ListExp*
ListString	::=	*String*
	|	*String* , *ListString*
ListRHS	::=	*RHS*
	|	*RHS* | *ListRHS*
RHS	::=	*ListItem*
MinimumSize	::=	nonempty
	|	ϵ
Reg2	::=	*Reg2 Reg3*
	|	*Reg3*
Reg1	::=	*Reg1* | *Reg2*
	|	*Reg2* - *Reg2*
	|	*Reg2*
Reg3	::=	*Reg3* *
	|	*Reg3* +
	|	*Reg3* ?
	|	eps
	|	*Char*
	|	[*String*]
	|	{ *String* }
	|	digit
	|	letter
	|	upper
	|	lower
	|	char
	|	(*Reg*)
Reg	::=	*Reg1*
ListIdent	::=	*Ident*
	|	*Ident* , *ListIdent*

Appendix B

Some JVM Instructions

These tables contain all instructions used in Chapters 5 and 6 and some other ones that can be useful as optimizations in Assignment 4. We use the dot (.) to separate values on the stack, and two-letter variables (*dd,ee*) to represent double values. The asterisk (*) in an explanation indicates that there is a longer explanation after the tables.

Jasmin	args	stack	explanation	HEX
aload	var i	$. \rightarrow .V(i)$	load ref from var i	19
aload_i (i=0..3)		$. \rightarrow .V(i)$		2A..2D
areturn		$.r \rightarrow$	return ref from method	B0
astore	var i	$.r \rightarrow .$	store ref in var i	3A
astore_i (i=0..3)		$.r \rightarrow .$	store ref in var i	4B..4E
bipush	byte i	$. \rightarrow .i$	push byte i as int	10
d2i		$.dd \rightarrow .i$	convert double to int	8E
dadd		$.dd.ee \rightarrow .dd + ee$	add double	63
dcmpg		$.dd.ee \rightarrow .i$	compare if $>$*	98
dcmpl		$.dd.ee \rightarrow .i$	compare if $<$*	97
dconst_dd (dd=0,1)		$. \rightarrow .dd$	push double	0E,0F
ddiv		$.dd.ee \rightarrow .dd/ee$	divide double	6F
dload	var i	$. \rightarrow .V(i)$	load double from var i	18
dload_i (i=0..3)		$. \rightarrow .V(i)$	load double from var i	26..29
dmul		$.dd.ee \rightarrow .dd * ee$	multiply double	6B
dneg		$.dd \rightarrow . - dd$	negate double	77
dreturn		$.dd \rightarrow$	return double from method	AF
dstore	byte i	$.dd \rightarrow .$	store double in var i	39
dstore_i (i=0..3)		$.dd \rightarrow .$	store double in var i	47..4A
dsub		$.dd.ee \rightarrow .dd - ee$	subtract double	67
dup		$.v \rightarrow .v.v$	duplicate top (for int)	59
dup2		$.dd \rightarrow .dd.dd$	duplicate top (for double)*	5C

Jasmin	args	stack	explanation	HEX
goto	label L		go to label L	A7
i2d		$.i \rightarrow .dd$	convert int to double	87
iadd		$.v.u \rightarrow .v + u$	add int	60
iconst_m1		$. \rightarrow . - 1$	push int constant -1	02
iconst_i (i=0..5)		$. \rightarrow .i$	push int constant	03..08
idiv		$.v.u \rightarrow .v/u$	divide int	6C
if_icmpeq..le	label L	$.v.u \rightarrow .$	compare ints on stack*	9F..A4
ifeq..le	label L	$.v \rightarrow .$	compare int with 0*	99..9E
iinc	var i, byte c		increment var i with c	84
iload	ref i	$. \rightarrow .V(i)$	load int from var i	15
iload_i (i=0..3)		$. \rightarrow .V(i)$	load int from var i	1A..1D
imul		$.v.u \rightarrow .v * u$	multiply int	68
ineg		$.v \rightarrow . - v$	negate int	74
invokestatic	method	$.v...w \rightarrow .$	call static method	B8
invokevirtual	method	$.v...w \rightarrow .$	call virtual method	B6
irem		$.v.u \rightarrow .v\%u$	remainder int	70
ireturn		$.v \rightarrow$	return int from method	AC
istore	ref i	$.v \rightarrow .$	store int in var i	36
istore_i (i=0..3)		$.v \rightarrow .$	store int in var i	3B..3E
isub		$.v.u \rightarrow .v - u$	subtract int	64
ldc	int v	$. \rightarrow .v$	push int constant v*	12
ldc2_w	double dd	$. \rightarrow .dd$	push double constant dd*	14
nop			do nothing	00
pop		$.v \rightarrow .$	pop int	57
pop2		$.dd \rightarrow .$	pop double*	58
return		$. \rightarrow$	return void from method	B1

More explanations:

- dcmpg, dcmpl: the value left on the stack is 1 if the inequality holds, 0 if the values are equal, and -1 otherwise.

- dup2: the instruction duplicates the topmost two words, which can be one double value or two integer values.

- if_icmpeq, if_icmpne, if_icmplt, if_icmpge, if_icmpgt, if_icmple corresponding to $=, \neq, <, \geq, >, \leq$ jump to the label if the comparison holds between the top-2 integer values on the stack.

- ifeq, ifne, iflt, ifge, ifgt, ifle corresponding to $=, \neq, <, \geq, >, \leq$ jump to the label if the comparison holds between the top integer value on the stack and 0.

- ldc, ldc2_w: the constants pushed are stored in the constant pool, and the actual bytecode argument (after assembly) is a reference to this pool.

- pop2: the instruction pops the topmost two words, which can be one double value or two integer values.

Appendix C

Summary of the Assignments

The full specifications of the assignments can be found on the book web page, together with supporting material such as test suites and code templates.

Assignment 1: Parser for C++

Write a parser for a fragment of the C++ programming language. This fragment is defined by "real-world" code from the web page of the book *Accelerated C++* by Koenig and Moo. The parser should return an abstract syntax tree at success and report an error with a line number at failure.

The recommended implementation is via a BNF grammar processed by the BNF Converter (BNFC) tool. The approximate size of the grammar is 100 rules. With BNFC, no more files than the grammar have to be written.

Assignment 2: Type Checker for CPP

Write a type checker for a fragment of C++. The type checker should print an "OK" at success and report a type error at failure. The syntax of the language is specified in Section 2.10, and its type system is explained in Chapter 4.

The recommended implementation is via BNFC and some general-purpose language. The syntax tree created by the parser is processed further by a program using the skeleton generated by BNFC. The approximate size of the grammar is 50 rules. The type checker code is around 150–300 lines, depending on the programming language used.

Assignment 3: Interpreter for CPP

Write an interpreter for a fragment of C++. The interpreter should run programs and correctly perform all their input and output actions. The language is the same as in Assignment 2. The interpreter should follow the semantic rules specified in Chapter 5.

The recommended implementation is via BNFC and a general-purpose language. The syntax tree created by the parser is first type checked by using the type checker created in Assignment 2. The interpreter should then make another pass of the code. The interpreter code is around 150–300 lines.

Assignment 4: Code Generator for CPP

Write a code generator for a fragment of C++. The code generator should correctly translate programs into Java class files, by first generating Jasmin assembly code and then converting it to JVM bytecode with the Jasmin program. The language is the same as in Assignments 2 and 3.

The recommended implementation is via BNFC and a general-purpose language. The syntax tree is first type checked; adding type annotations is recommended here, if not previously done in Assignment 2. The code generator should then make a pass of the type-annotated tree. Around 250–300 lines of code are needed.

Assignment 5: Interpreter for Fun

Write an interpreter for the small untyped functional programming language explained in Chapter 7. The interpreter should walk through programs and print out the value of the **main** function. It should implement both call-by-value and call-by-name strategies, which are selected by a command-line flag.

The approximate size of the grammar is 15 rules. The interpreter code is around 100 lines, depending on the programming language used.

Assignment 6: A Special-Purpose Language

Design and implement a query language. The language should cover an adequate set of queries in some domain. The implementation should parse queries and return answers. The solution should include complete source code and documentation, which includes a human-readable grammar, a user manual, and a **Makefile** for compiling the system.

The syntax can resemble a formal or a natural language, e.g. SQL or English. The implementation can use BNFC or GF. Also an embedded language is allowed, but the host language tools (such as a Haskell interpreter) must be hidden from the user. The expected size of the language is 50–100 abstract syntax rules, thus about three times the size of the language in Section 8.10. It should cover infinitely many different queries. The answering engine can be a database, a web service, or a program such as a mathematical problem solver.

Appendix D

Further Reading

This is a highly personal reading list, presenting my favourites rather than a balanced literature survey. But it strongly reflects the sources that inspired this book. The book web page http://digitalgrammars.com/ipl-book/ gives links to the material that is available on-line.

Chapter 1.

> A. Aho, R. Sethi, M. Lam, J. Ullman, *Compilers Principles, Techniques & Tools*, Second Edition, Pearson Education, 2007.

also known as the *Dragon Book*, is the classic compiler book. Its nickname comes from the cover picture, where a knight is fighting a dragon entitled "Complexity of Compiler Design" with "LALR Parser Generation" as her (his?) sword and "Syntax-Directed Translation" as her shield. These concepts are central in the current book as well—but the 1009 pages of the Dragon Book also show how they work under the hood, and they cover advanced topics such as parallelism.

> A. Appel, *Modern Compiler Implementation in ML/C/Java*, Cambridge University Press, 1998.

also known as the *Tiger Book*, is another thorough book on compilers—actually a set of three books with a common theory part. Its main impact on this book is the idea that the same theoretical ideas can be encoded in different programming languages. These books are indeed rich in theory, in particular about modern optimization techniques and dataflow analysis.

> R. Sebesta, *Concepts of Programming Languages*, Ninth Edition, Pearson Education, 2010.

covers the history and classification of programming languages, with entertaining interviews of creators of C++, Java, Perl, and many other languages.

> D. Knuth, *Selected Papers on Computer Languages*, CSLI Publications, 2003.

is a rich source on the earliest and most fundamental ideas, including Knuth's original paper on LR(k) parsing.

Chapter 2. Appel's book triple mentioned at Chapter 1 was a direct inspiration to BNFC, showing how the same set of concepts can be implemented in different languages.

> T. Parr, *The Definitive ANTLR Reference: Building Domain-Specific Languages*, Pragmatic Programmers, 2007.

is another high-level grammar formalism, whose exact relation to BNFC remains to be defined. It uses a version of LL parsing.

> A. Koenig and B. Moo, *Accelerated C++*, Addison-Wesley, 2000.

is the source of the code examples defining the fragment addressed in Assignment 1. It is an unusual book on C++, focusing on the high-level aspects of the language and the use of the Standard Template Library almost as an embedded language.

Chapter 3. The Dragon and Tiger books (Chapter 1) cover the details needed for implementing lexer and parser generators. But

> J. Hopcroft, R. Motwani, and J. Ullman, *Introduction to Automata Theory, Languages, and Computation*, Second Edition, Addison-Wesley, 2001.

is the classic book on formal language theory and its relation to computability. It gives all details of the algorithms, including proofs of correctness.

Chapter 4.

> B. Pierce, *Types and Programming Languages*, The MIT Press, 2002.

is the classic book on type systems in programming languages.

> S. Thompson, *Type Theory and Functional Programming*, Addison-Wesley, 1991. Also available on-line.

explores the limits of what can be done with types, including specifications and proofs of programs.

Chapter 5.

> M. Fernández, *Programming Languages And Operational Semantics: An Introduction*, King's College Publications, 2004.

is an accessible introduction to operational semantics, using them to characterize precisely the differences between programming paradigms.

> B. Kernighan and K. Ritchie, *C Programming Language (2nd Edition)*, Prentice-Hall, 1988.

in addition to being both a brief yet deep introduction to C, is a major source of insight in how data is stored and how memory management works.

Chapter 6.

> T. Lindholm and F. Yellin, *The Java Virtual Machine Specification*, Second Edition, Addison-Wesley, 1999. Also available on-line.

is the definitive source for JVM instructions, also giving hints on how to compile to it.

> T. Downing and J. Meyer, *Java Virtual Machine*, O'Reilly, 1998.

explains the workings of JVM and a way to generate it by using the Jasmin assembler.

> P. Carter, *PC Assembly Language*, 2006. Available on-line.

is both brief and deep, and a major source in how machines work. It is free and it comes with a set of tools helping to use the NASM assembler to actually produce code that runs on your computer platform.

> R. Stallman, *Using and Porting the GNU Compiler Collection*, Free Software Foundation, 1988–2008. Available on-line

is a detailed explanation of how GCC works.

> *The LLVM Compiler Infrastructure*, `llvm.org/`.

may be making all other current ways to produce machine code obsolete.

Chapter 7.

> J. Peyton-Jones and D. Lester, *Implementing Functional Languages: a Tutorial*, Prentice-Hall, 1992. Available on-line.

is a hands-on book on compiling lazy functional languages to machine code, and the source of many ideas in Chapter 7.

> M. Jones, Typing Haskell in Haskell, *Proceedings of the 1999 Haskell Workshop, Paris*, 1999. Available on-line.

is a thorough, yet easily readable article (for those who know Haskell, at least). The type checker in Section 7.9 can be seen as a simplified version of the code presented in this paper.

> X. Leroy, Compiling Functional Languages, *Spring School "Semantics of Programming Languages", Agay*, 2002. Available on-line.

is a compact introduction to both interpreters, code generation, and optimization of functional languages, from the creator of OCaml.

Chapter 8.

> P. Graham, *Hackers & Painters*, O'Reilly, 2004. Essays also available on-line.

inspired a lot of the material in this chapter. For instance, it includes a discussion of what programming languages will look like a hundred years from now (i.e. from 2003).

> E. Raymond, *The Art of Unix Programming*, Prentice-Hall, 2003. A version available on-line.

was another source which, in particular, advocates the creation of "mini-languages" as a programming technique, and gives surveys of many such languages.

> Wikipedia article "Lambda calculus",
> `en.wikipedia.org/wiki/Lambda_calculus`.

was an important source for Section 8.2, and

Wikipedia article "Brainfuck", en.wikipedia.org/wiki/Brainfuck.

for Section 8.3.

B. Stroustrup, *The Design and Evolution of C++*, Addison-Wesley, 1994.

gives a balanced view on the trade-offs faced when trying to raise the level of a language and at the same time keep it efficient and attractive to main-stream programmers. Written by the creator of C++, it is honest about design flaws, many of which were detected when it was too late to fix them, because so many people had started using the flawed constructs in their code.

T. Parr, *Language Implementation Patterns: Create Your Own Domain-Specific and General Programming Languages*, Pragmatic Programmers, 2009.

is a guide to developing domain-specific languages using the ANTLR tool (see Chapter 2 above).

Wolfram Alpha, Computational Knowledge Engine, wolframalpha.com.

is a natural-language query system with knowledge of both mathematics and trivia.

G. Hutton, Higher-order functions for parsing, *Journal of Functional Programming* 2(3), pp. 323–343, 1992. Available on-line.

was our source for parser combinators in Haskell.

A. Ranta, *Grammatical Framework: Programming with Multilingual Grammars*, CSLI Publications, 2011.

is a book about GF, which was used for implementing the query language in English and Haskell. GF and BNFC share many ideas. Their common mission is to make language implementation more accessible by the use of code generation from grammars. The GF book and the current book were partly written in parallel.

Index

Lightning Source UK Ltd.
Milton Keynes UK
UKHW050116261119
354195UK00021B/950/P